Coffee with Calvin

Also by Donald K. McKim

The Church: Its Early Life
The Authority and Interpretation of the Bible: An Historical Approach
    (with Jack B. Rogers)
The Authoritative Word: Essays on the Nature of Scripture (editor)
Readings in Calvin's Theology (editor)
What Christians Believe about the Bible
*A Guide to Contemporary Hermeneutics: Major Trends in Biblical
    Interpretation* (editor)
How Karl Barth Changed My Mind (editor)
Ramism in William Perkins' Theology
Theological Turning Points: Major Issues in Christian Thought
Major Themes in the Reformed Tradition (editor)
Encyclopedia of the Reformed Faith (editor)
Kerygma: The Bible and Theology (4 volumes)
The Bible in Theology and Preaching
Westminster Dictionary of Theological Terms
God Never Forgets: Faith, Hope, and Alzheimer's Disease (editor)
Historical Handbook of Major Biblical Interpreters (editor)
Historical Dictionary of Reformed Churches (with Robert Benedetto
    and Darrell L. Guder)
Calvin's Institutes: Abridged Edition (editor)
*Introducing the Reformed Faith: Biblical Revelation, Christian
    Tradition, Contemporary Significance*
The Westminster Handbook to Reformed Theology (editor)
The Cambridge Companion to Martin Luther (editor)
Presbyterian Beliefs: A Brief Introduction
Presbyterian Questions, Presbyterian Answers
The Cambridge Companion to John Calvin (editor)
Calvin and the Bible (editor)
Historical Dictionary of Reformed Churches, 2nd ed. (with Robert
    Benedetto)
Dictionary of Major Biblical Interpreters (editor)
*Ever a Vision: A Brief History of Pittsburgh Theological Seminary,
    1959–2009*
A Reformed Faith That Lives Today (Japanese translation)
More Presbyterian Questions, More Presbyterian Answers
A "Down and Dirty" Guide to Theology

DONALD K. McKIM

Coffee with Calvin

Daily Devotions

WESTMINSTER
JOHN KNOX PRESS
LOUISVILLE · KENTUCKY

First edition
Published by Westminster John Knox Press
Louisville, Kentucky

13 14 15 16 17 18 19 20 21 22 — 10 9 8 7 6 5 4 3 2

Book design by Drew Stevens
Cover design by Lisa Buckley
Cover illustration: Coffee © *violetkaipa/shutterstock.com*

Library of Congress Cataloging-in-Publication Data

McKim, Donald K.
    Coffee with Calvin : daily devotions / Don McKim. -- 1st ed.
        p. cm.
    Includes bibliographical references.
    ISBN 978-0-664-23681-6 (alk. paper)
    1. Calvin, Jean, 1509–1564. Institutio Christianae religionis.
    2. Meditations. I. Title.
    BX9420.I69M35 2013
    230'.42 — dc23

                                                    2012032923

♾ The paper used in this publication meets the minimum requirements of the American National Standard for Information Sciences — Permanence of Paper for Printed Library Materials, ANSI Z39.48-1992.

Most Westminster John Knox Press books are available at special quantity discounts when purchased in bulk by corporations, organizations, and special-interest groups. For more information, please e-mail SpecialSales@wjkbooks.com.

Madeline Ogden McKim

May she learn appreciatively from John Calvin

CONTENTS

3. Following God's Way

4. Helps for the Christian Life

5. Living as a Christian

6. When Times Are Good

7. When Times Are Bad

8. Anticipating the Future

PREFACE

I have long wanted to write a Calvin devotional book.

To some, this may seem like a strange notion. Or impossible. To think of John Calvin (1509–1564), the "master of Geneva," is to conjure images of a cold, heartless, rationalistic theologian; an adherent of predestination, which turned God into a tyrant. The common cultural image of Calvin does not lend itself to a book of excerpts from his writings that are meant to nourish Christian faith and devotion.

But those who study Calvin know better. To immerse oneself in Calvin's writings is to enter a theological field rich with insights into Scripture and Christian theology. It is to explore what these sources can mean for the church and the lives of Christians. Calvin was an eminently practical theologian. He believed theology should be not just a matter of the head, but also of the heart and the hands as well. Our theological understandings of the God revealed in Scripture deepen and strengthen our faith. They call us to give all praise to the God of our salvation and all commitment to the Christ who is our Lord and Savior. All this happens by the power of the Holy Spirit.

My hope is that these short extracts from Calvin and my comments on them will introduce Calvin's theological insights. But even more, I hope that they will help us find how these insights can strengthen, challenge, and nourish Christian faith. My passion is for Calvin's thoughts to become valued helps for Christian living among those who know Calvin now in varying degrees and for those for whom some coffee with Calvin will be their first conversation with this important theologian.

For Calvin, theological insight and piety go hand in hand. One without the other is not complete. So to read Calvin devotionally is also to read Calvin theologically. And vice versa. I hope this volume will serve both purposes.

I have written eighty-four devotions for this book. They are divided into eight sections with seven, or a multiple of seven, devotions in each segment. This is to make it easy to use this book devotionally during a series of weeks.

The titles of the sections indicate the type of topics in each. The first section on "Basics of Christian Belief" looks at major theological ideas in Calvin's thought and what they mean. Section 2, "Life in the Church," shows the importance of the church as the place and the way in which our Christian experience takes shape. Section 3, "Following God's Way," orients us to the life of faith and its basic elements. Section 4, "Helps for the Christian Life," considers the meanings of theological topics as ways of assisting us in our lives of faith. The long section 5, "Living as a Christian," contains a number of topics that are dimensions of the Christian life and form the fiber and core of who we are as disciples of Jesus Christ. The devotions in section 6 are for when times are good, whereas those in section 7 are for when times are bad. The final section focuses our attention on "Anticipating the Future," with meditations on resurrection and the life to come. The sections are all interrelated and the topics are porous in relation to each other. No matter where we start in Calvin's theology and in his devotional dimensions, we work our way through the various loci, or places, of theology to circle around the whole of Christian theological beliefs.

This book can be used in a daily fashion, reading through each section, in any order. It can also, of course, be picked up for occasional use at any time. Wherever one dips into Calvin's thought, there is much to be understood and appropriated for Christian life and service. Given the profound nature of Calvin's thought, I suggest these devotions be read slowly, taking time to reflect on each sentence.

The selections in this book are all drawn from Calvin's great theological work, the *Institutes of the Christian Religion* (Latin, 1559). There are wonderful treasures in this work, as I hope these devotions will show. There are many more treasures to be found in Calvin's exposition of Scripture, his biblical commentaries, and his sermons. Perhaps later volumes can mine the penetrating and nourishing insights that emerged as Calvin faithfully interpreted the Bible.

The selections from the *Institutes* are the focus of each devotion. When quotes are given without a Calvin reference, they are from the selection at the top of the page. Other quotes are cited with reference to the book, chapter, and section of the *Institutes*. There are a number of Calvin quotes in the devotions since I've tried to let Calvin speak for himself as much as possible.

I have used the translation of Calvin's *Institutes* from Ford Lewis Battles, a Calvin scholar without peer. He was my revered teacher at Pittsburgh Theological Seminary and through his work he also introduced readers to Calvin's piety (Latin *pietas*), that "reverence joined with love of God which the knowledge of his benefits induces" (*Institutes* 1.2.1; see Ford Lewis Battles, *The Piety of John Calvin: A Collection of His Spiritual Prose, Poems, and Hymns* [1978; repr., Phillipsburg, NJ: P & R Publishing, 2009]). Our devotion to God in Christ emerges from the knowledge of God we have in the Gospel in which the benefits of Jesus Christ are given to us. Our devotion, or piety, is a proper reverence and love for this God who has first loved us.

Battles's translation does not reflect today's usage of inclusive language for humans or contemporary concerns about the language used for God. I have retained the original translation as found in the Library of Christian Classics edition of the *Institutes*, but I have used inclusive language in my comments on Calvin's texts and in relation to God.

May these devotions enhance our theological understandings and our piety. If I may paraphrase and make personal Calvin's comment: For not only does piety beget reverence toward God, but the very sweetness and delightfulness of

God's grace so fills us who are cast down in ourselves with fear, and at the same time with admiration, that we depend upon God and humbly submit ourselves to God's power (*Institutes* 3.2.23).

Donald K. McKim

Germantown, Tennessee
Eastertide 2012

ACKNOWLEDGMENTS

The title of this book coincides with an interesting Website by George Moseley of Collierville, Tennessee, at http://www.coffeewithcalvin.com. The blog posts are Moseley's comments on reading Calvin's *Institutes of the Christian Religion*, begun during 2009, the 500th anniversary year of Calvin's birth. See also the Facebook page for discussions: http://www.facebook.com/pages/Coffee-With-Calvin/271977069144. Moseley has been innovative and creative in giving Calvin's thought a wider audience and I am grateful for his efforts.

My thanks are due to Westminster John Knox Press for accepting this project for publication, especially to Editorial Director, David Dobson, and also to Jana Riess for excellent and perceptive editorial comments, which were most helpful. Erika Lundbom and Julie Tonini worked on the manuscript with their usual great skill.

Through the years, a number of teachers of Calvin's thought —and other scholars and friends—have continued to deepen my interest and passion for Calvin. This worldwide Calvinian community makes Calvin resources available, for which we can be most appreciative.

My first book on Calvin, *Readings in Calvin's Theology* (1984), was dedicated to our young sons, Stephen and Karl. Now they are grown and married. LindaJo and I rejoice in our wider family of Stephen and Caroline, and Karl and Lauren. When the final writing for this book was being completed in 2010,

Stephen and Caroline welcomed the birth of their daughter, Madeline Ogden McKim. We rejoice! I dedicate this book to her and renew my hope expressed in the dedication of the earlier book to Maddie's father and uncle: May she "learn appreciatively from John Calvin."

1. Basics
of Christian Belief

1. Scripture: Our Spectacles

Just as old or bleary-eyed men and those with weak vision, if you thrust before them a most beautiful volume, even if they recognize it to be some sort of writing, yet can scarcely construe two words, but with the aid of spectacles will begin to read distinctly; so Scripture, gathering up the otherwise confused knowledge of God in our minds, having dispersed our dullness, clearly shows us the true God. (*Institutes* 1.6.1)

The Bible is a pair of eyeglasses, spectacles to snap into clarity the "confused knowledge of God in our minds." We may not think of the Bible with this image, but it is an important one.

Calvin believed that humans are born with an innate knowledge of God. We know intuitively within ourselves that there is a God who exists and stands behind all things, including us ourselves (1.3–4).

But this knowledge of God is not something we gravitate toward and love. The Scriptures teach that we reject this knowledge of God, rebel against it. Instead of helping us know God, this knowledge of God leads to our being inexcusable in God's sight (1.4–5; Rom. 1). We deserve God's judgment for rejecting our Creator in our lives. This is the power of sin. Sin destroys our ability to know God through nature or the things around us.

But God has given us the Bible to show us who God is and what God does. The Bible enables us to see the creation around us as the work of God. So to come to know God truly, we need "another and better help" (1.6.1).

The Bible is the spectacles that give us the "pure and clear knowledge of God" that we cannot gain from any other place (1.5.15). The Bible "clearly shows us the true God," for in Scripture God "opens his own most hallowed lips" (1.6.1).

2. Trinity

Furthermore, this distinction is so far from contravening the utterly simple unity of God as to permit us to prove from it that the Son is one God with the Father because he shares with the Father one and the same Spirit; and that the Spirit is not something other than the Father and different from the Son, because he is the Spirit of the Father and the Son. (*Institutes* 1.13.19)

Calvin wrote much about the Trinity. God is one God who is at the same time three persons: Father, Son, and Holy Spirit.

The Trinity is a core of Christian belief, distinguishing Christian faith from other religions that believe in many gods, or simply in one god as a single, solitary unit. For Calvin, the doctrine is taught in Scripture, though the term *Trinity* does not occur in Scripture (1.13.3).

Recognizing the unity and the diversities in the Trinity is helpful and meaningful for us. When we are baptized, says Calvin, we are baptized into the name of the one God, as Christ commanded (1.13.16; Matt. 28:16–20). There is one God, one Lord who claims our lives. It is to this God that all worship and honor and obedience is due.

Yet this one God is also three distinct persons, each fully God and each with work to perform. Calvin wrote "to the Father is attributed the beginning of activity, and the fountain and wellspring of all things; to the Son, wisdom, counsel, and the ordered disposition of all things; but to the Spirit is assigned the power and efficacy of that activity" (1.13.18).

While we do not fully understand the Trinity, we worship the triune God, the "great one in three," as the hymn "Holy, Holy, Holy" puts it. But we can know God as Father, Son, and Holy Spirit within our lives. Thanks be to God!

3. Creation: Theater of God's Glory

Let us not be ashamed to take pious delight in the works of God open and manifest in this most beautiful theater. (*Institutes* 1.14.20)

Calvin often referred to the heavens and the earth, the works of God, as a theater in which the creator's glory can be seen (1.5.8; 1.6.2; 2.6.2). This most beautiful theater enables faith to see that "wherever we cast our eyes, all things they meet are works of God" (1.14.20).

The eyes of faith can see this. Calvin recognizes that because of sin, our "whole knowledge of God the Creator" turns out to be "useless unless faith also followed, setting forth for us God our Father in Christ." While the "universe should be the school in which we were to learn piety, and from it pass over to eternal life," sin has ruined this scenario (2.6.1).

But to those who have faith and know that God the Creator is also God the Redeemer in Jesus Christ, the "heavens are telling the glory of God; and the firmament proclaims his handiwork" (Ps. 19:1). We can take the "pious delight in the works of God" of which Calvin speaks.

We can find such joys in nature! We know God the Creator is the source of it all, for "the earth is the Lord's and all that is in it" (Ps. 24:1). So praise and thanksgiving for the wonderful theater of nature is a Christian impulse, always.

But humans who enjoy this "dazzling theater" (1.5.8) also have responsibilities to care for the good creation. Our concerns for the environment and ecology are grounded in gratitude to the good Creator and are for the purposes for which all things are created.

Praise God! Preserve the earth!

4. Providence

Gratitude of mind for the favorable outcome of things, patience in adversity, and also incredible freedom from worry about the future all necessarily follow upon this knowledge. (*Institutes* 1.17.7)

God's providence is God's carrying out what God has eternally decided to do in all things, according to Calvin (see 1.16.8). Calvin has a very robust view of this doctrine, seeing it applied to the whole of nature and life, to human decisions, and to the ultimate course of history. He wants to leave no role for fortune or chance, but to see that all things are ordained by God.

Calvin's views on the comprehensiveness of providence have not been persuasive to all people. But Calvin sees belief in God's providence as sustaining us in both good times and bad. He wrote "ignorance of providence is the ultimate of all miseries; the highest blessedness lies in the knowledge of it" (1.17.11).

Providence makes us grateful. All we have and are comes from God. God cares for us and loves us. We experience God's "beneficence," says Calvin, as we recognize the ways God blesses us (1.17.7).

In adversity we can be patient, trusting God's will and purposes to work for good (see Rom. 8:28). When we suffer injustice or miseries, or even destruction, our faith remains.

Most practically, providence frees us from worry about the future. Calvin enumerated a number of calamities common in his day. We can create our own list. But no fears are fatal if we believe that even when "the world appears to be aimlessly tumbled about, the Lord is everywhere at work" (1.17.11). We can trust that God's work will be for our welfare. This is the great comfort and hope of God's providence for us and for our world.

5. Sin

The whole man is overwhelmed—as by a deluge—from head to foot, so that no part is immune from sin and all that proceeds from him is to be imputed to sin. As Paul says, all turnings of the thoughts to the flesh are enmities against God [Rom. 8:7], and are therefore death [Rom. 8:6]. (*Institutes* 2.1.9)

We cannot imagine a grimmer picture of humans than what Calvin paints here in light of his reading of Paul. Through his whole theology, Calvin maintains this view of humanity, a view he believed was rooted in Scripture.

There is a pervasiveness of sin through all life. Calvin's image is head to foot, so there is no part that is immune from sin and whatever proceeds from us is to be imputed, or attributed, to sin. Later theologians called this total depravity. It is not that people are depraved in the sense of being totally dangerous. Rather, sin affects our whole selves, all dimensions—heart, will, mind. We are sinful in the totality of our lives. We are sinners by nature, and sin is comprehensive in scope.

Our only hope for help is if God provides it. God has and does in Jesus Christ. God saves us sinners when we cannot help ourselves at all. Sin makes us turn away from God completely. God gives salvation, doing for us what we cannot do for ourselves. God elects or predestines us to salvation, purely by grace, since we cannot save ourselves, says Calvin.

As believers in Christ, we know that we still sin. We seek God's forgiveness daily. Now that we are in Christ, sin does not rule in us completely. But sin is real. The only answer: confess our sin and repent always. God continues to forgive us. God restores us in love. For this, great thanksgiving!

6. Common Grace

If we regard the Spirit of God as the sole fountain of truth, we shall neither reject the truth itself, nor despise it wherever it shall appear, unless we wish to dishonor the Spirit of God. (*Institutes* 2.2.15)

Some Christians believe that anything around us that does not originate from Christian people or that is part of secular culture is necessarily sinful and should be avoided. They see a strong dichotomy between nature and grace, between things done by Christian people and things done by those who do not have Christian faith.

But Calvin had a wider view. He believed God's common grace provided that, despite human sin, there are natural gifts given to humans that can develop and flourish. These include talents in arts and sciences, the ability to construct civil government, and the grace to live in enough harmony in society so that complete chaos and destruction does not ensue.

This general or common grace is different from God's "special grace," which is the grace given in salvation (2.2.17). Common grace originates from the Spirit of God so that human societies may function with good and important social purposes being carried out. This is a blessing for Christians and non-Christians alike.

Calvin's followers have appreciated and participated in the arts, sciences, government, and causes that enhance human life. We can join with others, whoever they are or whatever they believe, to work for common aims and purposes. We receive the benefits that others not of our faith provide us in all areas of life. So full participation in society and receiving whatever good society can provide is important. We can follow truth from whatever source since it ultimately comes from the Spirit of God.

We are grateful for God's grace upholding our world and good blessings from many sources.

7. Christ the Mediator

Now it was of the greatest importance for us that he who was to be our Mediator be both true God and true man. . . . His task was so to restore us to God's grace as to make of the children of men, children of God; of the heirs of Gehenna, heirs of the Heavenly Kingdom. (*Institutes* 2.12.1,2).

Jesus Christ stands at the center of our Christian faith. From the early centuries the church believed it was important to recognize the uniqueness of who Jesus was and what he did.

The church maintains Jesus is truly human, truly divine. He was both God and human at the same time. Both dimensions are crucial for the most important task in the world: human salvation.

In Christ, God restored us as humans to the relationship that God intended to have with us from the start: trusting, loving, and obeying God. Human sin broke this relationship. But in Jesus Christ, we have new life! As the mediator between God and humanity, Christ has restored us to God's grace, transforming us from children of sin to children of God, from persons set to oppose God to "heirs of the Heavenly Kingdom."

As fully divine and fully human, Jesus our mediator can bring this grace as no other person can do. Through his death and resurrection, the power of sin is defeated and he is our Redeemer. As a person like us in all ways except sin (Heb. 4:15), Jesus takes on our human life, knowing us fully, and saving us as who we are, the children of sin.

This is the wonderful news of the Gospel! Christ is our mediator, standing between God and us, and by his work transforms us into the children of God, heirs of God's kingdom.

8. Salvation

We have in his death the complete fulfillment of salvation, for through it we are reconciled to God, his righteous judgment is satisfied, the curse is removed, and the penalty paid in full. (*Institutes* 2.16.13)

Our salvation is centered in Jesus Christ. Christ is the one who lived and died and was raised to save us.

Calvin captures this by recognizing that in the death of Christ, salvation is fulfilled. He lists biblical images, one after another, to point to the fullness of what Christ has done to make salvation possible. Through his death we receive reconciliation with God and our relationship is repaired. Through Christ, God's righteous judgment is satisfied since Christ, who is sinless, has died for our sins. Through Christ, the curse of sin is removed since his death completely covers our sin and the sin of the world. Through Christ, the penalty is paid in full. That is, the results of sin that should fall on us—judgment and death—have fallen on Christ. With all this, says Calvin, we have in Christ's death complete salvation.

Calvin goes on to say that it is in Christ's resurrection that he "came forth victor over death, so the victory of our faith over death lies in his resurrection alone" (2.16.13). Christ's resurrection gives his death its "power and efficacy in us" (2.16.13). What happened on the cross is vindicated by the resurrection.

Christ's death and resurrection go together. They bring us the wondrous salvation we receive as God's gracious gift. Jesus Christ has done for us what we cannot do for ourselves. Through his death and resurrection, we receive forgiveness of sins and eternal life. Our relationship with God in Christ by the power of the Holy Spirit begins now and lasts forever. Thanks be to God!

9. The Holy Spirit

The Holy Spirit is the bond by which Christ effectually unites us to himself.... Faith is the principal work of the Holy Spirit. . . . Paul shows the Spirit to be the inner teacher by whose effort the promise of salvation penetrates into our minds, a promise that would otherwise only strike the air or beat upon our ears. . . . Faith itself has no other source than the Spirit. (*Institutes* 3.1.1,4)

The work of the Holy Spirit, the third person of the Trinity, is great and magnificent. The Spirit unites us to Jesus Christ in a bond that never breaks. The Spirit establishes this bond by faith.

We may not often recognize it, but our faith in Jesus Christ as Lord and Savior is by the work of the Holy Spirit in us. We come to faith by God's gracious work in granting the Spirit to enable us to believe. This is the Spirit's principal work, says Calvin. He cites Paul to say the Spirit is our inner teacher who makes the promise of salvation real, penetrating our minds. Without the Spirit, the promise would only "strike the air or beat upon our ears."

What a comfort to realize our faith is not self-generated. Salvation is God's gift of grace through the Spirit! We need never fear that our faith will "fail" because God's Spirit will not fail. The source of faith is the Spirit, which means that our faith is not based on ourselves or our own abilities. It is a free gift from the Holy Spirit of God who is at work within us. No more restless nights worrying about whether we are good enough or doing enough to merit faith. Faith is grounded in the Spirit who gives faith and sustains faith. We can rest in this assurance.

10. Eternal Life

For before their [believers'] eyes will be that day when the Lord will receive his faithful people into the peace of his Kingdom, "will wipe away every tear from their eyes" [Rev. 7:17; cf. Isa. 25:8], will clothe them with "a robe of glory . . . and rejoicing" [Ecclus. (Sir.) 6:31, EV], will feed them with the unspeakable sweetness of his delights, will elevate them to his sublime fellowship—in fine, will deign to make them sharers in his happiness. (*Institutes* 3.9.6)

Whenever we face troubles in life, said Calvin, we should be aroused "to meditate upon the future life" (3.9.1). We may love this present world too much, so our heart becomes "occupied with avarice, ambition, and lust, [and] is so weighed down that it cannot rise up higher." Indeed, our "whole soul" may get so caught up in the "allurements of the flesh" that it "seeks its happiness on earth" (3.9.1).

Yet, while we should be thankful for God's kindness to us on earth (3.9.3), we also should desire the better life of heaven, of eternal life. Heaven is our "homeland," said Calvin, where "to enjoy the presence of God is the summit of happiness" (3.9.4).

In spite of what happens in this life, and in spite of all the wickedness that flourishes, there is the comfort of the life to come, to which we can look. Calvin is rhapsodic in trying to describe what we will find in the peace of God's kingdom: no tears, clothed in glory, being fed with God's unspeakably sweet delights, sublime fellowship. Altogether, we will be sharers in God's divine happiness. We have only the smallest glimpse of the ultimate glories of eternal life in God's presence, praising God's glory with all the saints. This is our eternal home, our everlasting joy!

11. Justification

> Therefore, we explain justification simply as the accep-
> tance with which God receives us into his favor as righ-
> teous men. And we say that it consists in the remission
> of sins and the imputation of Christ's righteousness.
> (*Institutes* 3.11.2)

A major New Testament image for salvation is justification. This is a special theme throughout Romans where Paul speaks of being "justified by faith" (Rom. 5:1) and describes the results that emerge from justification.

Calvin, too, found justification a key way to describe the Christian's relationship to God. He calls justification "the main hinge on which religion turns" (3.11.1). Justification is necessary because of the seriousness of sin. For Calvin, sinners stand under the judgment of God. They face the consequences of their sinfulness in light of their iniquity, which is "abominable to God, so no sinner can find favor in his eyes" (3.11.2).

In justification, the sinner becomes righteous in God's sight. The sinner can stand "firm before God's judgment seat" (3.11.2). This justification takes place through Jesus Christ. Christ imparts his righteousness (as a sinless person) to the sinner. The sinner receives Christ's righteousness by faith. Justification is by faith so that the sinner, clothed in Christ's righteousness, "appears in God's sight not as a sinner" but as a righteous person (3.11.2).

This leads to Calvin's simple declaration of justification as acceptance in which God receives us into God's favor as righteous persons. This means our sins are forgiven; and we receive the imputation, or giving of Christ's righteousness, as our own.

Justification by faith was a vital insight for Luther and for Calvin. Our salvation is by faith; we are righteous in God's sight by the work of Christ received in humble trust. No good works can save us; only Christ's work that we receive in faith.

12. Union with Christ

That joining together of Head and members, that indwelling of Christ in our hearts—in short, that mystical union—are accorded by us the highest degree of importance, so that Christ, having been made ours, makes us sharers with him in the gifts with which he has been endowed. (*Institutes* 3.11.10)

We grow in faith by the work of the Holy Spirit in us. We experience the Spirit as we are in union with Christ (3.1.1).

This is an important concept in Calvin's theology. Without being united with Christ by faith, all the work of Christ would be for nothing. We could not benefit from it (3.14.4). In our experience of salvation, in justification, we are drawn into the closest possible relationship with Christ in the bond of faith.

Calvin speaks of the "indwelling of Christ in our hearts" so we share in the "gifts with which he has been endowed." Being engrafted into Christ's body makes us one with him. Christ "grows more and more into one body with us, until he becomes completely one with us" (3.2.24). We are "participants not only in all his benefits but also in himself" (3.2.24). Calvin calls this a mystical union, not meaning that humans are absorbed into the divine, but that believers participate in Jesus Christ by faith and are united with him in the deepest spiritual bond. This is a "bond of fellowship," which gives us a "wonderful communion, day by day" (3.2.24).

What could be more precious to us than this wonderful communion shared with Jesus Christ? We are united with him in the strongest bonds. Calvin said, "there is no sanctification apart from communion with Christ" (3.14.3). Our gradual transformation and growth in faith is by the Spirit within us as we participate in Christ.

13. Sanctification

Christ justifies no one whom he does not at the same time sanctify. These benefits are joined together in an everlasting and indissoluble bond, so that those whom he illumines by his wisdom, he redeems; those whom he redeems, he justifies; those whom he justifies, he sanctifies. (*Institutes* 3.16.1)

Being set right with God in justification is accompanied by being "sanctified by Christ's spirit" so we may "cultivate blamelessness and purity of life." Justification and sanctification go together. They are "double grace" (3.11.1).

Sanctification is our growth in faith, our doing of good works and being led by the Spirit of God within us as we serve God in the church. We are reconciled to God in Christ by faith alone. We may distinguish justification and sanctification. But Christ "bestows both of them at the same time, the one never without the other" (3.16.1).

In sanctification, we are "summoned to holiness" and "aroused to love" (3.16.2). We love God and serve God, loving and serving others—doing that to which God calls us by the Spirit. Our actions do not gain us merit or provide the means to salvation. Christ is the only source of our justification. But Christ is our "example in order that we may follow his footsteps [1 Peter 2:21]." "If we cleave to Christ" we are "members of one body [1 Cor. 6:15, 17; 12:12], who must help one another in our mutual tasks [cf. 1 Cor. 12:25]" (3.16.2). All this is "that God may be glorified in us [Matt. 5:16]."

Here is good news: The God who justifies us is with us as we live our faith in sanctification. Double grace is ours!

14. Election in Christ

But if we have been chosen in him, we shall not find assurance of our election in ourselves; and not even in God the Father, if we conceive him as severed from his Son. Christ, then, is the mirror wherein we must, and without self-deception may, contemplate our own election. (*Institutes* 3.24.5)

Calvin is always associated with election or predestination. Caricatures of his views abound. Many have disagreed with Calvin's views, from his times to the present. To his opponents, election seems to be a doctrine that robs people of their decision-making abilities and is unfair in not giving everyone a chance to be saved.

This was not Calvin's intention and not the emphasis in his views. He saw God's election as a doctrine of comfort. It assures believers that our salvation does not rest on our own decisions or abilities, but on God's gracious choosing of us to receive salvation as a gift. Our sin has left us unable to choose to accept Christ or move toward God in faith. To such sinners, God chooses to give salvation in Christ. Our assurance of election comes when we look at Christ—as in a mirror—and ask, Do I believe in Jesus Christ? If we are in communion with Christ, we have a "sufficiently clear and firm testimony that we have been inscribed in the book of life" (3.24.3). For Calvin it is key that we see Jesus Christ as the mirror of election. He is the one in whom we are chosen and through whom salvation comes to us.

We need have no sleepless nights wondering if we are saved. Our election or salvation has a human face: the face of Jesus. If we believe in him, our election is assured. What comfort!

2. Life in the Church

15. The Communion of Saints

> It is as if one said that the saints are gathered into the
> society of Christ on the principle that whatever benefits
> God confers upon them, they should in turn share with
> one another. (*Institutes* 4.1.3)

There's an odd phrase in the Apostles' Creed that is often passed over lightly when we recite it. "I believe in the communion of saints." What does it mean?

The saints are all those who are part of the holy catholic Church, the phrase that comes immediately before this one in the creed. *Saints* is the biblical term for Christian believers, appearing in the plural in the New Testament. They are the multitude of believers from the earliest days onward—those who believed in God's promises as part of the people of Israel and now, those who believe in Jesus Christ. The saints are the people of God. They are the great "cloud of witnesses" (Heb. 12:1), or the elect of God, in Calvin's terms.

The saints are one through their common faith in Jesus Christ. They are, says Calvin, gathered into the society of Christ. This is our true identity as Christians and where we find our true home—along with other saints, in the society of Christ, the Christian church. We are not lone rangers in our faith; we join with others in the communion of saints, in the body of Christ.

We receive the benefits of believing in Christ, with others in the church. But our communion with other saints obligates us also to pass along what we have been given. We should share with one another, says Calvin, what God confers on us. God's grace should be extended to others. God's love, mercy, care, justice, peace—all the benefits we receive as saints—are to be conveyed to others in the society of Christ.

The benefits and obligations of believing in Christ are very real. They comfort us and challenge us to receive and give what has come to us.

16. Church as Mother

For there is no other way to enter into life unless this mother conceive us in her womb, give us birth, nourish us at her breast, and lastly, unless she keep us under her care and guidance until, putting off mortal flesh, we become like the angels [Matt. 22:30]. Our weakness does not allow us to be dismissed from her school until we have been pupils all our lives. (*Institutes* 4.1.4)

We think of the church in many ways. It is more than the building we enter on Sunday. The church is people. We are the "society of God," as Calvin said, "the society of Christ" and the "communion of saints" (4.1.3).

Do we ever think of the church as mother? Calvin opens this image to convey, in the tenderest terms, how necessary the church is for us. Our mother will "conceive us in her womb, give us birth, and nourish us," then will keep us in her care and guide us. The visible church does the same. We can imagine no more essential or endearing image of our need for the church and what it provides throughout our lives.

From birth until death we cannot do without the church. We are pupils in the school of the church. Away from the church there is no hope of forgiveness of sins or salvation. The church is not an option for us. It is an absolute necessity. So Calvin said, "it is always disastrous to leave the church" (4.1.4).

We may take the church for granted or think we don't need it. But through the church God becomes present to us. The church is the mother of believers. We give thanks for our entering life and being sustained in the life of faith by the church.

17. Visible and Invisible Church

The church includes not only the saints presently living on earth, but all the elect from the beginning of the
world. Often, however, the name "church" designates
the whole multitude of men spread over the earth who
profess to worship one God and Christ. (*Institutes* 4.1.7)

To speak of the church theologically, we need to distinguish
two ways the term is used in Scripture. These are the invisible
church and the visible church.

Calvin distinguishes the church nobody except God sees
(invisible) from the church that everybody sees (visible). The
invisible church is all the elect of God from the beginning of the
world. They are believers in Jesus Christ who are "children of
God by grace of adoption and true members of Christ by sanctification of the Holy Spirit" (4.1.7).

The visible church is those who here and now "profess to
worship one God and Christ." In this church, said Calvin, are
"mingled many hypocrites who have nothing of Christ but the
name and outward appearance" (4.1.7).

So we can understand that the church may fail to be all God
wants it to be. For church people and their activities do not
always truly reflect the will of Jesus Christ. Calvin said in the
visible church there are "very many ambitious, greedy, envious
persons, evil speakers, and some of quite unclean life" (4.1.7).

This is not a flattering picture! Some who profess Christ do
not live in Christ's ways. Yet, we are "commanded to revere
and keep communion" with the visible church. We do not judge
whose profession is real. This is God's prerogative. Calvin quoted
Augustine: "Many sheep are without, and many wolves are
within" (4.1.8). We are to render a charitable judgment toward
others and honor their profession of faith. May we do so!

18. Worship

Believers have no greater help than public worship, for by it God raises his own folk upward step by step. (*Institutes* 4.1.5)

Our lives in the church are marked by a primary emphasis: worship.

The worship of God is a main response of biblical people in both the Old and New Testaments. The people of Israel were warned in the Ten Commandments not to bow down or worship idols, and that "you shall have no other gods before me" (Exod. 20:3).

But worship arises not out of fear but out of gratitude and praise. The Psalms are supremely intended for the worship of God, no matter what our mood or circumstances. "Worship the LORD with gladness; come into his presence with singing" (Ps. 100:2), proclaims the psalmist.

Calvin was concerned for the true and right worship of God, recognizing that "believers have no greater help than public worship." He made this comment in relation to David's desire to come to the Temple (Ps. 84:2–3). Worship was central to the lives of the Old Testament saints and it is equally so for Christian believers. For by public worship, "God raises his own folk upward step by step" (4.1.5). Worship is one of the great means of grace by which we live as God's people in the church, meaning the whole multitude of people "who profess to worship one God and Christ" (4.1.7).

Worship is not an option. It is an absolute necessity. Worship is foundational to our lives in the church. Through worship we offer praise and thanks to God who by the Spirit raises us up, step by step. Worship is a continuing activity as God's Spirit works within the church and in us. Let us worship God!

19. An Indivisible Connection

"The church, bathed in the light of the Lord, extends over the whole earth: yet there is one light diffused everywhere" [Cyprian]. Nothing more fitting could be said to express this indivisible connection which all members of Christ have with one another. (*Institutes* 4.2.6)

Calvin, like Paul, strongly emphasized the unity of the church (Eph. 4:5), grounded in its head, Jesus Christ (4.2.4; Eph. 1:22; 4:15). Despite all the differences and diversities, the church is one.

Early church theologian Cyprian wrote powerfully on the unity of the church. Calvin quotes him at length as Cyprian uses the image of "many rays of the sun but one light, and many branches of a tree but one strong trunk." If we break a branch from the tree, no sprouts can come. If a stream is cut off from its source, "it dries up" (4.2.6). Then, while the church, "bathed in the light of the Lord, extends over the whole earth: yet there is one light diffused everywhere." Cyprian's image is most fitting, said Calvin. It expresses this indivisible connection that all believers share.

Those who break the church apart by schism are detestable, said Calvin (4.1.5). Sisters and brothers in Christ have an indivisible connection with each other grounded in Jesus Christ, the head of the church. We sever relationships at our peril.

At the same time, believers in Christ are united with each other by a bond that will not break. The bond of love and fellowship in the church is a theological connection that cannot be broken by any human powers. It is deeper than all else.

The church is throughout the world. Wherever we are, we are connected by bonds of love with other believers. What a blessed fellowship!

20. The Likes of Us

The Lord has therefore bound his church together with a knot that he foresaw would be the strongest means of keeping unity, while he entrusted to men the teaching of salvation and everlasting life in order that through their hands it might be communicated to the rest. (*Institutes* 4.3.1)

God could rule in the world and the church all alone. God's word, which called into existence all there is, could as easily work in the church so that everyone would recognize and obey it.

But God does not choose to work that way. God uses humans to do God's work in the world and the church. God entrusts to us—such as we are—the "teaching of salvation and everlasting life" so through human hands, this might be "communicated to the rest" (4.3.1). God does not dwell with us visibly, said Calvin, but uses human ministers to declare God's will, "as a sort of delegated work" (4.3.1). Through their mouths, God's work is done, just as a worker uses a tool.

This is a great joy and challenge in ministry in the church. The joy is that God cuts us in on the action of ministry using *us* to help do God's will. The challenge is that we face our own limits and, most of all, our continuing sinfulness. We do not carry out God's will consistently or perfectly.

But love is the bond that unites the church, and it is in the ministries of the church—people working with people—that God's work can be done. The church can be bound together with the knot of the mutual love we have for each other, which comes from God's grace (Eph. 4:4–8, 10–16). This carries us through. Thank God we can do ministry—even the likes of us!

21. Doing Good Works

For we dream neither of a faith devoid of good works
nor of a justification that stands without them. . . . Faith
and good works must cleave together. (*Institutes* 3.16.1)

Both Martin Luther and John Calvin emphasized that we
are justified by faith alone and not by good works. This was
a basic Protestant understanding during the sixteenth-century
Reformation.

But while these reformers stressed that salvation is by faith
alone, they also recognized that justification is not by a faith
that is alone. That is, those who are justified by faith will seek
to do good works. This includes following God's law and living by love.

In the church, we recognize that while faith is the starting
point, good works follow. Without the works, faith cannot be
genuine. Without faith, good works will not save us. In the
spirit of Luther: Good works do not save a person, but a saved
person will do good works. This is captured in Calvin's dream of
neither "a faith devoid of good works nor of a justification that
stands without them." You can't have one without the other.

Good works are the expression of our salvation. We live
out our salvation in the church through the sanctifying work
of God's Holy Spirit. The church is the context in which what
we do in service of God in Christ takes shape. We never look at
what we do and think it merits God's favor or goodness. We live
out our faith, sharing love, seeking peace, pursuing justice—and
all other activities—as ways of expressing gratitude for grace
given and as ways of helping others in this world experience
God's love in Jesus Christ. God is pleased with "uprightness
and the duties of love" (3.4.36).

22. Loving God and Neighbor

> Hence it is very clear that we keep the commandments not by loving ourselves but by loving God and neighbor; that he lives the best and holiest life who lives and strives for himself as little as he can, and that no one lives in a worse or more evil manner than he who lives and strives for himself alone, and thinks about and seeks only his own advantage. (*Institutes* 2.8.54)

God's law, expressed in the Ten Commandments (Exod. 20), shows God's will for how we should live. The First Table indicates how we are to relate to God; the Second Table, how to relate to others through the "duties of love" (2.8.11). The commandments show that "first, indeed, our soul should be entirely filled with the love of God. From this will flow directly the love of neighbor" (2.8.51).

These perspectives guide Christians in the church. We live outer-directed lives. We worship and love God; we serve others, who are our neighbors. For Calvin, this means a turning away from self-love, which is at the root of sin. We are "too much inclined to self-love," which is an "excessive love" (2.8.54). Our primary focus in our lives of faith is not on ourselves, but toward God and others.

We are to strive for ourselves as little as we can. The worst kind of life and evil is when we strive for ourselves alone, thinking about and seeking only our own advantage. This is an image Luther used for sin: humans "turned in upon themselves." When we look in a mirror instead of out a window, we do not live in love as God desires.

We must be "ready to benefit our neighbor," said Calvin, "with no less eagerness, ardor, and care than ourselves" (2.8.54). Are we?

23. Loving All

We ought to embrace the whole human race without exception in a single feeling of love; here there is no distinction between barbarian and Greek, worthy and unworthy, friend and enemy, since all should be contemplated in God, not in themselves. . . . Whatever the character of the man, we must yet love him because we love God. (*Institutes* 2.8.55)

Calvin understood Jesus' parable of the Good Samaritan to show that the term *neighbor* includes even the most remote person. So "we are not expected to limit the precept of love to those in close relationships" (2.8.55; cf. Luke 10:36).

This comprehensive understanding of neighbor has far-reaching implications. It is a universal ethic that sees the duties of love are required of us toward all persons. Calvin indicates that the whole human race should be embraced in a single feeling of love. Everyone should be loved—without exception. Calvin shatters artificial divisions of nation, class, morality, even friend and enemy. All are to be loved; no qualifications are necessary!

The reason this is so and the theological grounding for it is that we contemplate others "in God, not in themselves." Our primary relationship is with God our creator who has also created all other persons. Thus our relationship with others is primarily a theological relationship. It is not based on choosing whom to love by some criteria, such as being of the same country, race, or family. We love indiscriminately because all others are related to God, just like we are.

Calvin is realistic in recognizing that if our decisions about whom to love were based on others alone, then these people would "more often engender hate than love" (2.8.55). But unchanging is the principle that no matter what someone's character, we love that person, because we love God. May we so live!

24. Abundant Grace

If we have faith in the Scriptures—which expressly proclaim that in Christ the grace and gentleness of the Lord have fully appeared, the riches of his mercy have been poured out [Titus 1:9; 3:4; II Tim. 1:9], and the reconciliation of God and men fulfilled [II Cor. 5:18ff.]—let us not doubt that the Heavenly Father's clemency flows forth to us much more abundantly, rather than that it is cut off or curtailed. (*Institutes* 4.1.26)

We live our Christian lives in the church, studying and listening to God's Word, participating in the sacraments, saying our prayers, loving others, and doing good works. But we still sin.

Sin is a reality for us in the church, no matter how deeply devoted we are to loving Jesus Christ. Can we obtain forgiveness, mercy?

Calvin reassures us that "God's kindness, which in the Old Testament had been unfailingly ready for the saints for the forgiveness of sins" (4.1.26) now continues for believers in Christ in the church. In Christ, the grace and gentleness of the Lord has fully appeared with his mercies.

What more wonderful image could we see? Now reconciliation between God and humanity has been fulfilled. Now God's "clemency flows forth to us" abundantly. The record of New Testament saints needing forgiveness—starting with Peter who denied Jesus—and continuing to groups in churches who lived disorderly lives, such as in Thessalonica, is that these saints are invited to repent (2 Thess. 3:14–15).

Even "the very order" of the Apostles' Creed, says Calvin, shows that there is "continual grace for sins . . . in Christ's church" (4.1.27).

What comfort and assurance we have in the forgiveness, mercy, and clemency of God. We receive abundant grace!

25. Prayer

This goal of prayer . . . namely, that hearts may be aroused and borne to God, whether to praise him or to beseech his help—from this we may understand that the essentials of prayer are set in the mind and heart, or rather that prayer itself is properly an emotion of the heart within, which is poured out and laid open before God, the searcher of hearts [cf. Rom. 8:27]. (*Institutes* 3.20.29)

For all Calvin's heavy theological discussions, the longest chapter in his *Institutes* is the one on prayer. Calvin sees prayer as absolutely essential for the Christian.

Prayer is simply "conversation with God," an "intimate conversation" (3.20.4,5). It is offered to the merciful God who "never either sleeps or idles" (3.20.3) and to the one in whom we can rest that "none of our ills is hid," who, "we are convinced, has both the will and the power to take the best care of us" (3.20.2).

Prayer does not take place alone. The Holy Spirit teaches us in prayer (3.20.5) and the risen Christ is our intercessor, the "Mediator, who should appear in our name and bear us upon his shoulders and hold us bound upon his breast so that we are heard in his person" (3.20.18).

This intimacy in prayer is amazing! The goal of prayer is to orient our hearts to God, as we seek God's help. We can be wholly honest in our prayers, pouring out our hearts before God in faith (3.20.11).

All this gives us great confidence to pray to God with the help of Jesus Christ and the Holy Spirit. Nothing is too small or unimportant that we cannot bring it to the Lord. Our deepest confidence is in the gracious God who hears and answers our prayers.

26. Word and Sign

Our merciful Lord, according to his infinite kindness, so tempers himself to our capacity that, since we are creatures who always creep on the ground, cleave to the flesh, and, do not think about or even conceive of anything spiritual, he condescends to lead us to himself even by these earthly elements, and to set before us in the flesh a mirror of spiritual blessings. (*Institutes* 4.14.3)

Our lives in the church are in constant need of nourishment and encouragement. Even having brothers and sisters in faith is not enough as means of ongoing support or as help in difficult times.

God nurtures our lives in the church by Word and sign, says Calvin. God's Word in Scripture, witnessing to Jesus Christ, communicates God's will to us and the message of the gospel. The signs God gives are the sacraments. They are signs of God's covenants. A sacrament is "an outward sign by which the Lord seals on our consciences the promises of his good will toward us in order to sustain the weakness of our faith" (4.14.1). Baptism and the Lord's Supper convey God's promises and confirm and seal the promises to us.

In infinite kindness, God gives Word and sign to prop up and sustain our "slight and feeble" faith (4.14.3). God uses earthly, common elements—water, bread, wine—to be mirrors of spiritual blessings. Word and sign go together. The word explains the sign and the sign confirms the word.

God ministers to us in our weakness. Word and sign convey the promises God gives to us. These promises become personal as we read and hear the Word of God and receive the sacraments that are "visible words" (Augustine) and that reflect all the spiritual blessings God gives to us.

27. Baptism

Baptism is the sign of the initiation by which we are received into the society of the church, in order that, engrafted in Christ, we may be reckoned among God's children. (*Institutes* 4.15.1)

Our entrance into the church is marked by baptism. Infants and adults are "engrafted in Christ" in baptism and united with Christ by faith. In baptism, we are welcomed into the community of the people of God, the church. In this reception and engrafting, we become "reckoned among God's children." We are adopted (Rom. 8:15) as God's children, members of the household of faith

Baptism is a sacrament, a sign and seal of our cleansing from sin. For "it is like a sealed document to confirm to us that all our sins are so abolished, remitted, and effaced that they can never come to his sight, be recalled or charged against us" (4.15.1). No matter when we are baptized, says Calvin, "we are once for all washed and purged for our whole life" (4.15.3).

This is how baptism has an ongoing effect for us. Even if we were baptized as infants we know that we were baptized and believe that the promises God makes to us in Christ are real and ongoing. Our sin can be continually cleansed and pardoned. Even when we sin or "fall away, we ought to recall the memory of our baptism and fortify our mind with it, that we may always be sure and confident of the forgiveness of sins" (4.15.3). Baptism took place for us once, but it affects us our whole life long. God gives us baptism to bring us into the family of God and receive God's forgiveness.

We thank God for our baptism and for being children of God in the church!

28. Lord's Supper

[God] has, through the hand of his only-begotten Son, given to his church another sacrament, that is, a spiritual banquet, wherein Christ attests himself to be the life-giving bread, upon which our souls feed unto true and blessed immortality [John 6:51]. (*Institutes* 4.17.1)

While our entrance into the church and adoption as children of God is marked by baptism, the Lord's Supper nurtures our faith in ongoing ways. We participate often in the Lord's Supper because we always need Jesus Christ, the life-giving bread. The Supper is a spiritual banquet in which we receive Jesus Christ himself. The bread and the wine are the outward elements that nourish us with the spiritual life-giving flesh and blood of our Lord and Savior.

This is a "high mystery," said Calvin. In the Supper we are continually supplied with "the food to sustain and preserve us in that life into which he has begotten us by his Word" (4.17.1). Nothing could be more personal or necessary than acts of eating and drinking. These actions in the Supper are means to receive the life-giving benefits of Jesus Christ, established in his life, death, and resurrection. In the Supper we are united with him by faith.

God gives us a visible expression of this mystery in Christ and our union with Christ by providing "visible signs best adapted to our small capacity" (4.17.1). This is how God works. God reaches out to us by providing just what we need—a visible expression of the deepest mystery we can know. Our lives are transformed through the work of Christ. This is real as we eat and drink in faith, receiving the body and blood of Christ.

The Lord's Supper is a joyful feast, a spiritual banquet giving us life—in Jesus Christ.

3. Following God's Way

29. The Holy Spirit Leads Us to Christ

As we cannot come to Christ unless we be drawn by the Spirit of God, so when we are drawn we are lifted up in mind and heart above our understanding. (*Institutes* 3.2.34)

Our journey in the Christian life starts with faith. At some point, we say yes to Jesus Christ as our Lord and Savior. We recognize our lives as engrafted to Christ and part of the body of Christ, the church. This happens through faith.

Calvin emphasizes that it is the Holy Spirit who gives the gift of faith. Through the Spirit we grasp "the mind of Christ" (1 Cor. 2:10). God gives the Spirit to bring people to Christ (John 6:44–45). Faith in Christ is not a matter of our human rationality, emotion, or experience. It is the gift of the Spirit of God, given by God in grace. This is why faith is such a source of gratitude for us. We know we do not deserve it and cannot attain it by ourselves. To believe in Christ is the result of God's total graciousness, giving to us the great gift of grace.

When we are drawn by the Spirit to believe in Christ, we are "lifted up in mind and heart above our understanding." We do not know why God has chosen us to have faith. We cannot use our own powers to unlock the mysteries of God's will.

At the same time, faith lifts us beyond our human understanding, giving us knowledge of God in Jesus Christ that we can attain in no other way. Faith takes us beyond human powers. The Spirit is our inner teacher who illuminates us with the greatest gift we can receive.

30. Faith Is a Matter of the Heart

For the Word of God is not received by faith if it flits about in the top of the brain, but when it takes root in the depth of the heart that it may be an invincible defense to withstand and drive off all the stratagems of temptation. (*Institutes* 3.2.36)

The Bible is the means God uses to convey faith in Christ to us, by the work of the Holy Spirit. In Scripture, we find the promises of God, focused in Christ (2 Cor. 1:20). We receive Scripture as God's Word by faith, just as we receive Jesus Christ as our Lord and Savior by faith, through the Spirit.

Calvin makes it clear that we need more than head knowledge of the Scriptures, a knowledge that "flits about in the top of the brain." We need a heart knowledge that is deeply rooted within us. This knowledge enables us to resist temptation through the Word of God.

This heart knowledge comes by the work of the Holy Spirit. The Spirit seals in our hearts "the very promises the certainty of which it has previously impressed upon our minds" (3.2.36). The Spirit guarantees Scripture promises by confirming and establishing them. This sealing with the Spirit "makes firm the gospel among us" (3.2.36; cf. 2 Cor. 1:21–22 and 2 Cor. 5:5).

It is the greatest comfort to know and believe the Gospel, realizing our trust in Scripture as God's revelation is not dependent on human arguments or logic, but on the Spirit of God. Our commitment to Scripture as the Word of God "takes root in the depth of the heart" and is enabled by the work of God's Holy Spirit. The Spirit gives us the deepest confidence in Scripture as God's divine communication to us.

31. Living in Faith and Hope

Hope is nothing else than the expectation of those things which faith has believed to have been truly promised by God. Thus, faith believes God to be true, hope awaits the time when his truth shall be manifested. . . . Faith is the foundation upon which hope rests, hope nourishes and sustains faith. (*Institutes* 3.2.42)

We live the Christian life by faith. Faith is God's gift to us by the Holy Spirit. In faith we believe in God and God's promises in Scripture, found fully in Jesus Christ.

At times, our faith may waver. We may go through periods when faith seems weak and even the promises of God feel far away.

Then, we also need hope. In faith, we hold on to God and God's promises. In hope we await the time when God's truth will be revealed to us. Calvin sees the closest bond between faith and hope. Without faith, our hope would be vacuous, nothing more than wishful thinking. Without "patient hope and expectation," our faith can "fail and grow faint." Paul "sets our salvation in hope [Rom. 8:24]. . . . Hope strengthens faith, that it may not waver in God's promises, or begin to doubt concerning their truth" (3.2.42). Hope is the ultimate future tense of faith. But hope pervades the present, keeping us in faith.

Succinctly, "hope refreshes faith, that it may not become weary" (3.2.42). God gives the gift of perseverance in faith, by hope. Hope "invigorates faith again and again" (3.2.42) that it may not become weary

Thank God for the gifts of faith and hope! We need them both. Now we can live confidently in the midst of all things that threaten.

32. Faith Leads to Repentance

With good reason, the sum of the gospel is held to consist in repentance and forgiveness of sins [Luke 24:47; Acts 5:31]. . . . That is, newness of life and free reconciliation . . . are conferred on us by Christ and both are attained through faith. . . . Repentance not only constantly follows faith, but is also born of faith. (*Institutes* 3.3.1)

Our faith in Jesus Christ leads us to repentance. Not once, but constantly.

For Calvin, "the sum of the gospel" is "repentance and forgiveness of sins." Central and crucial is that through the gospel of Jesus Christ, our sins are forgiven and we continually repent of sins we commit. This is the recipe for the Christian life. We are forgiven and repent; we repent and are forgiven.

These are the marks of the newness of life and free reconciliation that we receive. When we are forgiven, our new life is clear. When we sin, we are moved to repent of our sins because we are reconciled to God and are new creations in Jesus Christ (2 Cor. 5:17). This comes by the faith given to us by God through the Holy Spirit. Our faith allows us to receive forgiveness and moves us to repentance.

For Calvin, "repentance not only constantly follows faith, but is also born of faith." We do not repent in order to believe. This would turn repentance into work we do in order to receive something from God. But because we receive "pardon and forgiveness" through the "preaching of the gospel," we "cross over into the Kingdom of God" (3.3.1). In response, we break from the errors of our past life and apply our "whole effort to the practice of repentance." Repentance flows from faith and is "produced by it as fruit from a tree" (3.3.1). Repentance and forgiveness are our twin hopes!

33. The Race of Repentance

> I interpret repentance as regeneration, whose sole end is to restore in us the image of God that had been disfigured and all but obliterated through Adam's transgression. . . . God assigns to them a race of repentance, which they are to run throughout their lives. (*Institutes* 3.3.9)

Repentance marks our Christian lives. Over and over, we turn to God, seeking forgiveness of our sins. We are adopted children of God who experience God's love in Christ. But Christian believers are still sinners (3.3.10).

From God's point of view, the purpose of our repentance is "to restore in us the image of God that had been disfigured and all but obliterated through Adam's transgression." Repentance is regeneration in that we become new creations in Christ and are restored to the "original but ruined image of God" (from editor's note 17 in book 3, chapter 3 of the *Institutes*). The fellowship and trust and love of Adam and Eve to their creator (Genesis 1) is the goal of our regeneration—our being made new by the gift of faith in Jesus Christ.

But our Christian lives are always under construction. Indeed, we live in a race of repentance throughout our whole Christian lives. For this restoration in which God is engaged with us "does not take place in one moment or one day or one year; but through continual and sometimes even slow advances" (3.3.9). We must practice repentance throughout our lives and "know that this warfare will end only at death" (3.3.9).

Our race of repentance is real to us. We confess our sins and turn to God's ways, over and over. We need cleansing from guilt, the restoration of our minds and hearts to God's will. We are held in salvation by the "benefit of Christ" (3.3.9). But as we grow in faith we must also repent when we sin.

34. Down but Not Out

> God is said to purge his church of all sin, in that through baptism he promises that grace of deliverance, and fulfills it in his elect [Eph. 5:26–27]. . . . For the Spirit dispenses a power whereby they may gain the upper hand and become victors in the struggle. But sin ceases only to reign; it does not also cease to dwell in them. (*Institutes* 3.3.11)

Our experience in the Christian life brings victories and defeats.

The victories are those won by the power of the Holy Spirit within us, God's grace that enables us to live as Christian people. This is the ultimate victory over sin won by Jesus Christ and is signified in baptism, where we die and rise with Christ (Rom. 6:4). God regenerates us so "the sway of sin is abolished" in us, according to Calvin (3.3.11).

But we know defeats too. For while the "guilt of sin" is defeated, the "substance of sin" still remains in believers (3.3.11). The Spirit does provide a power so we may resist temptation and be assured of sin's forgiveness. But Calvin cautions that although sin no longer dominates us, it does not disappear. "Some vestiges remain," (3.3.11) says Calvin, to humble us by the consciousness of our own weakness. Our struggle with sin as Christians will be lifelong. Repenting of sin must be pursued "to the very end if we would abide in Christ" (3.3.20). Sin is down, but not out in our lives. We will never be perfect.

Yet ultimately sin does not hold terror. We are liberated from sin's guilt by the mercy of God. "Saints—otherwise deservedly sinners and guilty before God—are freed from this guilt" (3.3.11). Sin does cease to reign in us (Rom. 6:6). Praise God!

35. The Fruits of Repentance

Now we can understand the nature of the fruits of repentance: the duties of piety toward God, of charity toward men, and in the whole of life, holiness and purity. (*Institutes* 3.3.16)

Repentance is a "'turning of life to God'" (3.3.6). Repentance is "a singular gift of God" (3.3.21) expressing the pardon of our sin and our desire to walk in newness of life.

Our repentance should be shown by changes in our lives and in the fruits that our repentance brings. These are the expressions of our repentance. We do not do things to gain repentance; our repentance leads us to live, expressing the love we have for God in Christ, as these "mark sincere repentance" (3.3.16).

Calvin lists fruits of repentance as piety toward God, charity toward others, and holiness and purity in our lives. These embrace the two focal points of the Ten Commandments—our relationship with God and with others—as well as the motives and actions of our lives. Repentance leads us to a deeper worship and service to God, to a wider love toward others, and to lives of devotion and obedience to God. These are the directions our lives take as we desire to forsake sin and live as God desires.

But behind these actions is the nature of our hearts—what we love. For "when we have to deal with God nothing is achieved unless we begin from the inner disposition of the heart" (3.3.16; see Joel 2:13 and Jas. 4:8). This is key. All expressions of repentance (fruits) emerge from a heart given fully in devotion to God. As Calvin said, we must "cleanse away secret filth in order that an altar may be erected to God in the heart itself" (3.3.16).

May we bear fruits of repentance.

4. Helps for the Christian Life

36. Providence Brings Trust

Whence, I pray you, do they have this never-failing assurance but from knowing that, when the world appears to be aimlessly tumbled about, the Lord is everywhere at work, and from trusting that his work will be for their welfare? (*Institutes* 1.17.11)

Calvin's comprehensive view of providence provides that for the Christian, "the heart will not doubt that God's singular providence keeps watch to preserve it, and will not suffer anything to happen but what may turn out to its good and salvation" (1.17.6).

This sets us free from "the extreme anxiety and fear" that press us but also "from every care" (1.17.11). This assures us. It is based on God's promises as the one who governs all things, including the lives of each of us. This is of the greatest help in the Christian life. Many scriptural promises, such as "The Lord is my helper" (Ps. 118:6, 7) and that we may walk "in the midst of the shadow of death" (Ps. 23:4), bring us the deepest trust (1.17.11).

On the broader canvas of the world itself, we are assured that even when the world seems random, God is always at work. We may not see it. We may think things are bad and getting worse, or that God is an absentee landlord. But God's providential promises prevail. God is at work, even in an apparently aimless world.

For us, God's providence brings the trust that God's work will be for our welfare. Even when we are attacked by evil powers or evil persons, our times are in God's hands (Ps. 31:15) as are our lives. Indeed, "whatever changes take place from time to time," are "governed by God."

Providence brings trust and an assurance in which we may glory!

37. The Law as Help

The third and principal use [of the Law], which pertains more closely to the proper purpose of the law, finds its place among believers in whose hearts the Spirit of God already lives and reigns. . . . Here is the best instrument for them to learn more thoroughly each day the nature of the Lord's will to which they aspire, and to confirm them in the understanding of it. (*Institutes* 2.7.12)

The Law of God is the believer's friend!

This surprises us. The moral law is the impossible standard that we can never attain. We will always fall short of its demands. The law condemns us in our disobedience. Calvin says the law is like a "mirror. In it we contemplate our weakness, then the iniquity arising from this" (2.7.7). In itself, "the law can only accuse, condemn, and destroy" (2.7.7). Or, the law may be a deterrent. If we fear the consequences of breaking God's law, we will walk the line.

Both these dimensions are part of the law, as Calvin says. They breed fear. But Calvin develops a positive view. The law of God is the believer's friend and help. Its principal use is for Christian believers. The law of God expresses the will of God. It shows what God wants and how God wants us to live. From the "daily instruction of the law," we can "make fresh progress toward a purer knowledge of the divine will" (2.7.12).

For those in whom the Spirit of God lives and reigns, the desire to be obedient to God's will and way is super-strong. The law guides us in the "nature of the Lord's will" (2.7.12). It helps us. We can proclaim with the psalmist: "Oh, how I love your law!" (Ps. 119:97).

38. Faith Rests on God's Word

In understanding faith it is not merely a question of knowing that God exists, but also—and this especially—of knowing what is his will toward us. . . . We hold faith to be a knowledge of God's will toward us, perceived from his Word. (*Institutes* 3.2.6)

Christians are people of faith. We believe in Jesus Christ who is God with us, our Lord and Savior.

We know Jesus Christ—and the full revelation of God—through the Scriptures. They are the Word of God through whom Christ comes to us, "clothed with his gospel" (3.2.6). The Word, says Calvin, is "like a mirror in which faith may contemplate God" (3.2.6).

But faith is not primarily concerned in knowing that God exists. Rather, and especially, faith needs to know what God's will toward us is. This is a type of knowledge of God that relates God to us as humans; and as persons of faith.

The Scriptures help us by providing this knowledge of God. The Bible tells who God is and what God has done. Faith is receiving this "knowledge of God's will toward us, perceived from his Word."

This is why Bible reading is a key help for the Christian life. Through Scripture, our faith is strengthened and nourished as God's Word conveys God's will. We find direction for living as the Scriptures communicate God's will for us, supremely through Jesus Christ and his gospel. Here we contemplate God—in faith. The Holy Spirit enables the reading of Scripture to be the means by which our faith is given direction, bolstered, challenged, and energized. We hear God's Word, perceiving what God is saying and wants to do in our lives.

We proclaim, "Your word is a lamp to my feet and a light to my path" (Ps. 119:105).

39. Our Calling

> The Lord bids each one of us in all life's actions to look to his calling. . . . Lest through our stupidity and rashness everything be turned topsy-turvy, he has appointed duties for every man in his particular way of life. . . . Therefore each individual has his own kind of living assigned to him by the Lord as a sort of sentry post so that he may not heedlessly wander about throughout life. (*Institutes* 3.10.6)

If we were left on our own to determine what shape our Christian lives should take, where would we be?

We would probably be wandering around aimlessly, trying one thing and another, not sure of what we should be doing.

But God issues a calling for our lives. God calls us in election for salvation (3.24.1). God also calls us in our lives to be and to do. God calls us to activities in serving God that express our greater calling to salvation.

We often speak of "vocation" (from the Latin, *vocatio*, meaning "calling"). All Christians have this calling from God—to be disciples of Jesus Christ and live out our discipleship in word and deed. But God calls people to different ways of expression or tasks.

Usually we think of our vocation as connected with our work. This is a major way we serve God. But this does not mean that we need a paying job to live out our calling and have a shape to our Christian lives. Our duties, as Calvin calls them, can be in any situation or role—as parent, caregiver, or helper. Our vocation is who we are as well as what we do. Our work or role is like a sentry post, says Calvin, to give us a focus and a way of serving God.

Thank God for our vocation as we seek to serve!

40. The Comfort of Election

For just as those engulf themselves in a deadly abyss who, to make their election more certain, investigate God's eternal plan apart from his Word, so those who rightly and duly examine it as it is contained in his Word reap the inestimable fruit of comfort. (*Institutes* 3.24.4)

Thinking about election or predestination can be difficult, and for some it can even be unsettling. It is a doctrine associated with Calvin. But while he expounded it as the teaching of Scripture, he also recognized that this is a doctrine that, when it becomes a matter of speculation, can lead us into a "deadly abyss."

We worry about whether we are elect. What of others, are they?

Calvin's answer is always to look to Jesus Christ whom he calls "the mirror wherein we must, and without self-deception may, contemplate our own election" (3.24.5). We do not wonder about election apart from asking ourselves if we believe in Christ. In Christ, God's election is made clear. "Moreover," said Calvin, "when one comes to election, there mercy alone appears on every side" (3.24.1).

The emphasis should be on the inestimable fruit of comfort that election brings. Election means that we are saved by God's grace, not by our own choices or abilities. Our salvation is purely by God's gracious overture to us. For "God by his call manifests the election" which is otherwise hidden (3.24.1). We should, says Calvin, begin and end with God's call (3.24.4).

We have comfort in election because our salvation is secure in God's gracious mercy. Our response to God's call—to believe in Christ—is the outward expression of the election we see mirrored in Christ. Election has a human face, the face of Jesus Christ. This is the most immense comfort imaginable!

41. Forgiveness

> We must firmly believe that by God's generosity, medi-
> ated by Christ's merit, through the sanctification of the
> Spirit, sins have been and are daily pardoned to us who
> have been received and engrafted into the body of the
> church. (*Institutes* 4.1.21)

As Christians we know forgiveness is important. It marks our
first steps in the Christian life. As Calvin said, "Forgiveness of
sins, then, is for us the first entry into the church and Kingdom
of God. Without it, there is for us no covenant or bond with
God" (4.1.20). Forgiveness is an early expression of our faith.
In forgiveness we experience God's covenant love in Christ,
binding us to God and God to us.

God's forgiveness comes from God's generosity and involves
Christ through his merit and the sanctification of the Spirit. In
forgiveness the whole Trinity acts to pardon our sins. Forgiveness is possible from what Christ did in his death and resurrection. Forgiveness becomes real to us by the energy of the Holy
Spirit working within us.

Forgiveness of sin should happen daily since every day we
need God's forgiving power. We receive God's forgiveness since
we are "engrafted into the body of the church." Calvin noted
that "the Lord has promised his mercy solely in the communion
of saints" (4.1.20. cf. 22). In the church forgiveness becomes an
ongoing reality for the people of God. Without God's "constant
grace in forgiving our sins," said Calvin, "we shall scarcely abide
one moment in the church" (4.1.21). But since God has called us
to eternal salvation, we children of God "ought to ponder that
there is pardon ever ready" (4.1.21) for our sins.

We experience the sin/forgiveness pattern. We do not treat
God's forgiveness as automatic. We resist sin. But God pre-
serves and protects us by forgiving us.

42. God Is Ready to Forgive

The Lord requires the saints to confess their sins—and that indeed continually throughout life; and he promises pardon. . . . [God] . . . forgives not once or twice, but as often as men, stricken with the awareness of their transgressions, cry out to him. (*Institutes* 4.1.23)

We confess our sins daily because we are constantly in need of God's forgiveness. Our confession expresses our sorrow and remorse for what we have done. The Lord's Prayer reminds us, said Calvin, that as we daily pray the prayer, we daily "doubtless confess" (4.1.23) ourselves debtors when we pray, "forgive us our debts" (Matt. 6:12). We need to confess daily and "continually throughout life."

Our need is met by God's promise of pardon. There is pardon "ever ready" for our sins (4.1.21). In the Old Testament, as "promises of divine mercy are manifested in the Law and the Prophets toward the Israelites, so often does the Lord prove that he shows himself willing to forgive the offenses of his people" (4.1.24). In the New Testament, Jesus commanded his disciples to forgive others "seventy times seven" (see Matt. 18:21–22) so his disciples should "emulate [God's] kindness." Calvin assures us that God "forgives not once or twice," but as often as we are "stricken with the awareness" of our transgressions and cry out to God.

Calvin urges us to recognize God's willingness to forgive. God is more willing to forgive than we are to confess our sins. We are astounded to believe this! By ourselves, we would not be so willing to admit our sins. But the amazing message of the Gospel is that in Jesus Christ, "the grace and gentleness of the Lord" has "fully appeared" and "the riches of his mercy have been poured out [Titus 1:9; 3:4; II Tim. 1:9]." In him, God's "clemency flows forth to us" (4.1.26). In Jesus Christ we are forgiven.

5. Living as a Christian

43. Piety

I call "piety" that reverence joined with love of God which the knowledge of his benefits induces. For until men recognize that they owe everything to God, that they are nourished by his fatherly care, that he is the Author of their every good, that they should seek nothing beyond him—they will never yield him willing service. (*Institutes* 1.2.1)

The word *piety* has fallen on hard times. It has long been part of our theological heritage. But the caricatures of piety as a rigid, rule-oriented series of religious practices that have choked the vitality of faith have made the term suspect and often avoided. *Spirituality* is the current term for the God-given impulses of the Christian life.

But piety (Latin *pietas*) was key for Calvin, signifying what it truly means to know God. He wrote that "we shall not say that, properly speaking, God is known where there is no religion or piety" (1.2.1). His definition of *piety* as "that reverence joined with love of God which the knowledge of his benefits induces" is a comprehensive statement.

Piety is our response to what God has done—the benefits God has given. These are the benefits of Jesus Christ, found in the Gospel and in the whole story of salvation, found in the Old and New Testaments. Piety is reverence, acknowledging who God is as our creator. But this reverence is not a detached view of the transcendent. It is joined with love, which is our response to the God who has first loved us (1 John 4:7–21). We owe everything to God. We are nourished by God's parental care. We see God as the Author of our every good. We seek nothing beyond this magnificent God.

Piety is our attitudes and actions in living in the love God has given!

44. Listening to Scripture

We readily understand that we ought zealously to apply ourselves both to read and to hearken to Scripture if indeed we want to receive any gain and benefit from the Spirit of God. (*Institutes* 1.9.2)

Word and Spirit go together. God's Word in Scripture is the revelation of God's self to us. We recognize Scripture as the Word of God by the witness or testimony of the Holy Spirit (1.7.4–5). The Word helps us understand what God is saying to us through the Spirit. The Spirit makes the Word come alive for us as God's Word to us. As Calvin put it, "For by a kind of mutual bond the Lord has joined together the certainty of his Word and of his Spirit" (1.9.3).

So Scripture is central in our Christian lives. The Word is read and preached in worship and studied diligently by all Christians. Scripture is the means God uses to communicate to us by the Spirit. So we ought to not only read it but to heed it, said Calvin.

In a sense, we should be people of one book. Scripture is the source of our knowledge of God and forms the spinal column of our faith. We study Scripture using the best resources we can find, so that we can understand the Bible. We pray for God's Spirit to lead and guide us in interpreting Scripture as we use those resources so we may gain and benefit from what the Bible has to say to us. We ask the Spirit to apply the words of Scripture to our lives.

We study and listen to Scripture to hear God's Word to us.

45. See God in the Works of God

There is no doubt that the Lord would have us unin-
terruptedly occupied in this holy meditation; that, while
we contemplate in all creatures, as in mirrors, those
immense riches of his wisdom, justice, goodness, and
power, we should not merely run over them cursorily,
and, so to speak, with a fleeting glance; but we should
ponder them at length, and turn them over in our minds
seriously and faithfully, and recollect them repeatedly.
(*Institutes* 1.14.21)

For the Christian, the creation around us points to the creator
of all things (1.14.20). The beauty and greatness of creation are
seen by the eye of faith and become a source of praise for the
goodness of the creation and the Creator.

When we contemplate God's work in creation, we see what
we believe about who God is. The character of God is revealed
in faith so "God's inestimable wisdom, power, justice, and goodness shine forth in the fashioning of the universe." Indeed, "no
splendor, no ornament of speech, would be equal to an act of
such great magnitude" (1.14.21).

We should meditate on the creation. We should see "in all
creatures, as in mirrors, those immense riches" of God's wisdom, justice, goodness, and power. God's work reflects God's
self. We should look on creation, not with a fleeting glance,
but at length and recollect God's good creation repeatedly. We
know what it is that God is Creator, in true faith, when we "recognize God's powers in the creation of the universe" and apply
this knowledge to ourselves so our "very hearts are touched"
(1.14.21). The creation is not at arm's length from us. It causes
our hearts to sing! We see God's greatness and goodness in creation—leading to praise and worship, to thankfulness and trust.

46. All Salvation Is from God

> We see how, not simply content to have given God due praise for our salvation, he [the psalmist in Psalm 100:3] expressly excludes us from all participation in it. It is as if he were saying that not a whit remains to man to glory in, for the whole of salvation comes from God. (*Institutes* 2.3.6)

We owe our lives as Christians to the work of God. As in creation, we owe our existence to the God who made us (Ps. 100:3), so our salvation in Christ is purely by God's grace.

This is our great comfort! Our new life in Jesus Christ, our "regeneration, which is the beginning of the spiritual life," makes us a "new creation, which sweeps away everything of our common nature" (2.3.6). As sinners, we need a new nature, which God gives us in Jesus Christ (Eph. 2:10). As Calvin says, "our salvation is a free gift [cf. Eph. 2:5], because the beginning of every good is from the second creation, which we attain in Christ" (2.3.6).

We praise God for our salvation in Christ because all of salvation comes from God. This is a strong theological emphasis but also a strong devotional emphasis too. For God is "the author of spiritual life from beginning to end" (2.3.6). We do nothing to earn our salvation and we are excluded from all participation in it, says Calvin, interpreting Psalm 100:3 with the reading: "And we ourselves have not done it" (2.3.6). As we do not share in the creation of ourselves by God, so we do not share in any glory for our salvation—"not a whit," says Calvin.

The whole of salvation comes from God—beginning, middle, and end. God's grace in election saves and redeems us. All praise to God!

47. Live Blessedly and Die Happily

For they were then taught by a surer experience that the authority he wielded and the power he exercised were sufficient for believers not only to live blessedly but also to die happily. (*Institutes* 2.16.14)

We think often of Christ's death and resurrection. But how often do we think of his ascension?

The Apostles' Creed says, "he ascended into heaven." We recall that the disciples watched Jesus ascend until "a cloud took him out of their sight" (Acts 1:9). Today, we wonder how to interpret this.

Theologically, Christ's ascension is very important. Calvin says Christ "truly inaugurated his Kingdom only at his ascension into heaven" (2.16.14; cf. Eph. 4:10). Now Christ's presence is with us, wherever we are. He is not confined to an earthly body. Now we have the Holy Spirit with us too (John 16:7, 13–14).

This is all we need for the Christian life, isn't it? We experience the power of Jesus Christ in our lives, by the Holy Spirit. This is, for Calvin, the abundant help and blessing that carries us through our lives and brings us to death with a deep joy (2.16.14).

God's Spirit in Christ blesses us. Christ has ascended "so his power and energy were diffused and spread beyond all the bounds of heaven and earth" (2.6.14). The power we need for living is ours. It is the power of the risen and ascended Christ. This presence and power blesses us daily in all things. To live with a consciousness of Jesus Christ present with us in the here and now—what better blessing can there be?

We can live blessedly but also die happily. Our lives are hidden with Christ in God. We are secure now and in eternity. We do not fear. Praise the ascended Christ who is ever with us!

48. Faith

Now we shall possess a right definition of faith if we call it a firm and certain knowledge of God's benevolence toward us, founded upon the truth of the freely given promise in Christ, both revealed to our minds and sealed upon our hearts through the Holy Spirit. (*Institutes* 3.2.7)

We often wonder, What is faith? We speak about faith in different ways and senses. We have faith in many things—from our doctor to the brakes on our car. In the church, *faith* is a big word. What does it mean?

Calvin has a rich definition of faith as a "firm and certain knowledge." It is not empty or anti-intellectual, as if we need to turn off our brains when it comes to Christianity. This knowledge has a focus: on God's benevolence or good will toward us. Imagine that! God is for us and is generous and compassionate! This is hardly the wrathful, vengeful God we often hear about— sometimes, sadly, even in the church. We have an unshakable knowledge of God's goodness toward us. That's the kind of confidence we need for the living of our days.

How do we know this is God's attitude toward us? Simply from the promise in Christ. Jesus Christ shows us who God is and what God is like. In him is the promise that God is kind and merciful toward us. This promise can be believed. In Jesus we see how God deals with people like us—in love, with care, by mercy. Ultimately we see God's love in the death and resurrection of Jesus. God embraces us through the cross and then raises Jesus from the dead to assure us that our sin is forgiven and death's power is broken, forever. The Holy Spirit enables us to believe the promise of Christ with our minds and hearts, in the deepest dimensions of who we are.

This is faith: to believe in God's love for us, revealed in Christ, and made real by the Holy Spirit.

49. Christ's Death and Resurrection

> Therefore, we divide the substance of our salvation between Christ's death and resurrection as follows: through his death, sin was wiped out and death extinguished; through his resurrection righteousness was restored and life raised up, so that—thanks to his resurrection—his death manifested its power and efficacy in us. (*Institutes* 2.16.13)

The death and resurrection of Jesus Christ go together. Jesus' resurrection follows his death in the Gospels. Jesus' death is the necessary prelude to his resurrection. Theologically, each is important for salvation to occur.

Calvin indicates ways the death and resurrection of Christ are key for believers. Through Jesus' death, sin is obliterated and the power of death is broken. Somehow, through the death of Jesus, God forgives our sin and wipes away its power to hold us in its clutches. The ultimate result of sin—death—is snuffed out by the death of Christ. Jesus underwent death and through his death the power of death over us is taken away. This is why the cross is so central in Christianity. In the cross of Christ we find that sin's power is wiped out and death's power is extinguished.

The death of Christ has these effects because of Christ's resurrection. God raised Jesus from the dead so that Christ's death can have its sin-forgiving, death-defeating power. The resurrection established God's power in Christ over the powers of sin and evil, restoring righteousness for the world and raising Christ to new life so that from now on, new life for believers can be real. This is the celebration of Easter and all days when the resurrection of Christ is remembered. "Thanks to his resurrection," says Calvin, Christ's death works its power in us. Sin is forgiven; death is conquered. This is the glad news of salvation!

50. The Goal of Faith as God's Mercy

> Hope can have no other goal than faith has. But we have already explained very clearly that the single goal of faith is the mercy of God—to which it ought, so to speak, to look with both eyes. (*Institutes* 3.2.43)

Faith and hope are intimately related (3.2.42). Hope is, says Calvin, "nothing but the nourishment and strength of faith." In hope we "suspend our own desires until God's appointed time is revealed [Phil. 1:21]." We look for "the time when God will openly show that which is now hidden under hope" (3.2.43). This hope can push us forward; it gives us motivation and direction. Hope shapes our lives now.

As we look to the future, we live in the present, by faith. But present or future, hope and faith have the same goal. As we live in faith now, we look to faith's goal, which is "the mercy of God—to which it ought, so to speak, to look with both eyes." This is the hope we trust.

Now we live in faith, in the hope of salvation. We know we are sinners, so we rely on the mercy of God alone. We live "abandoning reliance upon works" (3.2.43) and depend on the one who will not deceive.

As we live daily, we anticipate the future, in hope. But day by day, as we live in faith we realize that what we need most is God's continuing mercy. We need forgiveness of sins and the power of the Holy Spirit to follow God's will and way for our lives. We live in hope of ultimate salvation, also based on God's mercy. No good works can earn mercy. God's mercy is freely given in Jesus Christ. To God's mercy we look in faith, now and forever.

51. Christ Our Example

Scripture shows that God the Father, as he has reconciled us to himself in his Christ [cf. II Cor. 5:18], has in him stamped for us the likeness [cf. Heb. 1:3] to which he would have us conform. (*Institutes* 3.6.3)

The foundation and fountain of the Christian life is what God has done in Jesus Christ.

Scripture shows, says Calvin, that God has "reconciled us to himself in his Christ." This is the central message of the Gospel and the event that enables us to be united with Jesus Christ by faith and experience our adoption as children of God (Rom. 8:15). Our sin is forgiven, we are justified by faith, and we experience the breaking of the power of sin that has ruptured our relationship with God, our Creator.

In Jesus Christ we see the likeness (image/imprint) of God (Heb. 1:3), to which God would have us conform, according to Calvin. We have "degenerated from the true origin and condition of our creation," by sin. But God in Christ provides the one "through whom we return into favor with God" and who is set before us as "an example, whose pattern we ought to express in our life" (3.6.3).

Jesus Christ is truly human, the church has said. He is the one to whom we look to see what it means to be a truly human person in God's sight. He is the model or example of what humans should be. Through his reconciliation by the cross and our adoption into the family of faith, he becomes the primary norm for our Christian lives. Our life is to "express Christ, the bond of our adoption" (3.6.3).

Jesus Christ is the guide for our Christian lives, the example who shows us how to live. We follow him.

52. The Inmost Affection of the Heart

> For it is a doctrine not of the tongue but of life. It is not apprehended by the understanding and memory alone, as other disciplines are, but it is received only when it possesses the whole soul, and finds a seat and resting place in the inmost affection of the heart. (*Institutes* 3.6.4)

There are many philosophies in which one may believe. Calvin was well aware of these in his day.

Over against them all is Christian faith. The Gospel of Jesus Christ is more than an intellectual activity. For Calvin, the Word of God "is not received by faith if it flits about in the top of our brain, but when it takes root in the depth of the heart" (3.2.36). He amplifies this when he says that the Gospel is "a doctrine not of the tongue but of life" (3.6.4). The Gospel of Christ we receive by faith is not a philosophy of life or interesting intellectual propositions. It is a life-changing reality that envelops the whole person. The Gospel transforms life from sin to faith. It affects the totality of who we are. Christian faith is more than merely something to be discussed. It is something to be lived!

The Gospel is truly received "only when it possesses the whole soul, and finds a seat and resting place in the inmost affection of the heart." All life is affected by the Gospel. Our commitment to Jesus Christ is total. We love him with our heart, soul, mind, and strength (Mark 12:30). The Gospel "must enter our heart and pass into our daily living, and so transform us into itself that it may not be unfruitful for us" (3.6.4). The Gospel impacts life and changes the inmost affection of our hearts.

53. We Are Not Our Own

We are not our own: let not our reason nor our will, therefore, sway our plans and deeds. We are not our own: let us therefore not set it as our goal to seek what is expedient for us according to the flesh. We are not our own: in so far as we can, let us therefore forget ourselves and all that is ours. (*Institutes* 3.7.1)

For Calvin, the sum of the Christian life is self-denial. Calvin cites Romans 12:1 as the duty of believers: to present their bodies as a living sacrifice to God. We are "consecrated and dedicated to God in order that we may thereafter think, speak, meditate, and do, nothing except to his glory" (3.7.1).

If so, then we recognize that we are not our own. In three sentences, all starting with "we are not our own," Calvin clarifies the implications of our theological and ethical commitment to God in Christ.

Our source of authority for decision making and action is not our own reason or will. Our goal in life is not to seek what is best for us. Since we are not our own, we must forget ourselves and all that is ours. This is focused dedication to handing over control of our lives from the control center that is us; to God. Since "we are God's," said Calvin, let God's "wisdom and will therefore rule all our actions." Since we are God's, "let us therefore live for him and die for him" (3.7.1).

Self-denial is our hardest command to obey. We relinquish what is natural for us, self-control, and present ourselves wholly to God. We depart from ourselves, said Calvin, so we can apply the "whole force" of our ability "in the service of the Lord" (3.7.1).

54. Dealing with God throughout Life

The Christian must surely be so disposed and minded that he feels within himself it is with God he has to deal throughout his life. In this way, as he will refer all he has to God's decision and judgment, so will he refer his whole intention of mind scrupulously to Him. (*Institutes* 3.7.2)

Our Christian lives are marked by recognizing that we deal with God throughout life. This is basic to us and distinguishes the life of faith from lives lived purely from ourselves and to ourselves.

The distinctiveness of faith is that as children of God and followers of Jesus Christ, we are led by the Spirit of God to see our lives as comprehensively related to God. This means, as Calvin notes, that we will refer all we have and are to God's decision and judgment. That is, we have given ourselves completely to God and seek God's will in all things. We wish our decisions to be toward what God wants of us and for us. We set the direction of our lives not in accord with our own wishes and desires, but with God's. We are thus orienting our intention of mind thoroughly and carefully toward God. All we do springs from our relationship with God in Jesus Christ. All we are reflects our dealings with God in which we deny ourselves and are dedicated to our Lord.

Dealing with God throughout life embraces the whole of the Christian life. It sets us to self-denial and toward seeking God's will and purposes for us. Denial of self means devotion to God. This is expressed throughout the totality of who we are—through our thoughts, desires, decisions, and actions. We recognize God's presence and see all things as related to God.

55. Humility

Whatever man we deal with, we shall treat him not only moderately and modestly but also cordially and as a friend. You will never attain true gentleness except by one path: a heart imbued with lowliness and with reverence for others. (*Institutes* 3.7.4)

Calvin believed our natural tendency is to be proud of ourselves and to "despise all others in comparison" (3.7.4). This is an expression of self-love, which, in a theological sense, is not good. We "burst with pride." We try to hide our vices from others while we "flatter ourselves with the pretense that they are slight and insignificant, and even sometimes embrace them as virtues" (3.7.4). Such are the lengths to which we go to flatter ourselves.

Yet, God enjoins us to "esteem and regard whatever gifts of God we see" in others so that we may honor them (3.7.4). This is God's call to humility. We should treat others "moderately and modestly but also cordially and as a friend." Our self-denial is thorough, giving up what we want to claim for ourselves and giving ourselves to humility in which we recognize God's gifts in others. We must relinquish everything that puffs us up and live with the humble attitude that gives proper honor to the gifts of others. This is more than being perfunctory. This humility should be the attitude of our hearts, enabling us to embrace others as friends. Calvin indicates that we will "never attain true gentleness except by one path: a heart imbued with lowliness and with reverence for others."

All our talents are the free gifts of God. They are not our own, so how can we boast (1 Cor. 4:7)? When we live in humility we honor the gifts God has given others, live in friendship, and show reverence for them.

56. Sharing All Benefits with Others

Whatever benefits we obtain from the Lord have been entrusted to us on this condition: that they be applied to the common good of the church. And therefore the lawful use of all benefits consists in a liberal and kindly sharing of them with others. (*Institutes* 3.7.5)

All we have comes from God. It is to be used for the common good of the church and shared with others.

This prescription shows us where our focus should be: on investing who we are and what we have for the sake of others. The benefits we have obtained have been entrusted to us for a purpose. They are not ours to hoard. They are ours to use for what God intends—that they be spread to others. As Calvin says, "no surer rule and no more valid exhortation to keep it could be devised than when we are taught that all the gifts we possess have been bestowed by God and entrusted to us on the condition that they be distributed for our neighbors' benefit [cf. 1 Peter 4:10]" (3.7.5).

So we recognize the obligations of our benefits. We do not live with closed arms to hold tightly to all we've been given. We are to live with open arms, to give and share. Calvin knew that this is hard for us. It goes against our grain. To do this means we must get out of ourselves. Nature so inclines us to the "love of ourselves alone that it does not easily allow us to neglect ourselves and our possessions in order to look to another's good" (3.7.5).

But we are to practice this "liberal and kindly sharing." The work of the church in mission and ministry can only happen when God's people do this. Will we?

57. Stewardship and the Rule of Love

> Let this, therefore, be our rule for generosity and benefi-
> cence: We are the stewards of everything God has con-
> ferred on us by which we are able to help our neighbor,
> and are required to render account of our stewardship.
> Moreover, the only right stewardship is that which is
> tested by the rule of love. (*Institutes* 3.7.5)

The word *stewardship* in the church is often too limited. It is usually tied to the church's finances and raising the church budget.
Hear the word *stewardship* and we reach for our checkbooks!

This is one proper dimension of stewardship. But it is not the
only dimension. Stewardship, as Calvin reminds, relates to the
fact that we are "stewards of everything God has conferred on
us" (3.7.5). All our resources come from God. As stewards, we
are those who manage God's resources responsibly.

All we have been given by God is to be used to help our
neighbor. This is the far-reaching concept that goes beyond giving money. We give much more—everything else that will help
our neighbor. As stewards, our lives are focused on generosity
and beneficence. We are generous with the resources God has
given because they are given to us to use for the sake of others.

Our stewardship is tested, says Calvin, by the rule of love.
Can we understand the ways that we are spending our money,
time, and energies as helping our neighbor and as an expression
of love? Are we looking primarily to the benefit of others rather
than to our own?

We are to "render account of our stewardship" of what we
have done with what we have been given. In the end, the rule of
love will be the test.

58. The Image of God in All People

> We are not to consider that men merit of themselves but to look upon the image of God in all men, to which we owe all honor and love. . . . Whatever man you meet who needs your aid, you have no reason to refuse to help him. Say, "He is a stranger"; but the Lord has given him a mark that ought to be familiar to you, by virtue of the fact that he forbids you to despise your own flesh [Isa. 58:7, Latin Vulgate]. (*Institutes* 3.7.6)

There is a bond that unites all people, regardless of the other distinctions we make in life—race, gender, religion, nationality. The bond is the image of God in which all people are created.

It's easy for us to mark the divisions among people. We create the distinctions and judge people by them. We may even judge by how good we think they are. But Calvin cautions that we should not fall into this. We are to "do good" to all (Heb. 13:16), no matter who they are. For they, like us, are created in the image of God. Not merit or worthiness but the simple fact that they are humans elicits our care and action.

This means we know no strangers. For this mark—the image of God, common to all—means that we do not hate or reject others because we would not hate or reject ourselves. When people provoke us or curse us, "not even this is just reason why you should cease to embrace him in love and to perform the duties of love on his behalf" (3.7.6). Seeing the image of God in others "cancels and effaces their transgressions, and with its beauty and dignity allures us to love and embrace them" (3.7.6). Will we see the image?

59. Devotion to God's Will

Scripture calls us to resign ourselves and all our possessions to the Lord's will, and to yield to him the desires of our hearts to be tamed and subjugated. (*Institutes* 3.7.8)

The ultimate expression of our love and devotion to God is "to resign ourselves and all our possessions to the Lord's will." This is the essence or "chief part of self-denial," as Calvin says. Self-denial "looks to God" (3.7.8).

How do we live a tranquil or convenient life? What is the best way to ride the waves of life? For Calvin the answer is to hand over all things to God. We give our lives and possessions and yield to God, "the desires of our hearts to be tamed and subjugated." This is what God calls us to do. It is the way we find the greatest joys in life: the blessings of God.

If we try to "heap up riches" our minds will always be unsettled. We may strive "to the point of weariness" to obtain our ambitions or avarice. Since "our lust is mad, our desire boundless," we can never rest easy (3.7.8).

Letting the Lord prosper us, in the denial of ourselves, is the way to live. God's blessing alone finds "a way, even through all hindrances, to bring all things to a happy and favorable outcome for us." We should never "desire nor hope for, nor contemplate, any other way of prospering than by the Lord's blessings" (3.7.8).

It is far better to trust God's plan for our lives than to try to enact our own plans, especially if we think that by our own skills and intelligence we can amass riches. Our single devotion should be to God's will. In denying ourselves, we look to God. Will we do so?

60. A Place to Rest and Plant Your Foot

For to have faith is not to waver, to vary, to be borne up and down, to hesitate, to be held in suspense, to vacillate—finally, to despair! Rather, to have faith is to strengthen the mind with constant assurance and perfect confidence, to have a place to rest and plant your foot [cf. 1 Cor. 2:5; 2 Cor. 13:4]. (*Institutes* 3.13.3)

If we look to ourselves for any source of comfort or assurance, we will be disappointed. As Christians, if we look to ourselves alone we will see our unrighteousness and know how far short we fall of what God desires for us. If we keep looking to ourselves, we will "at length despair." For we will realize "how great a weight of debt" is still pressed upon us and how far we stray from being who God wants us to be (3.13.3).

These kinds of self-examination—to find a clear conscience, hope, assurance or peace within—will surely fail.

But all is not lost! Our salvation is by faith, not by works. We receive faith as a gift, a faith based on God and not ourselves.

So Calvin encourages us not to despair. Our faith will not carry us through life only to leave us in anguish and gloom. Instead, despite all the zigs and zags, faith roots us in hopeful certainty. Assurance and confidence can be ours in the life of faith, even when our efforts are dismal. We can find rest and a strong foundation, a place to plant our foot in the assurances faith brings. Our confidence is in God and this is all we need!

61. Use Freedom for Others

We must at all times seek after love and look toward the edification of our neighbor . . . [1 Cor. 10:23–24]. . . . Nothing is plainer than this rule: that we should use our freedom if it results in the edification of our neighbor, but if it does not help our neighbor, then we should forgo it. (*Institutes* 3.19.12)

The Christian is free. We are free from many things because of Jesus Christ.

We are free from the law, not trusting in keeping the law for our salvation. As children of God in Christ we are free to obey the law now, to follow God's will as expressed in the law in joyful obedience. We are also free to use God's gifts for God's purposes. We use "the good things of God" and praise God for them (see 3.19.1–8).

While we have freedom in Christ, we also know that "'all things are lawful,' but not all things are beneficial" (1 Cor. 10:23). Calvin interprets this to mean that we are "at all times" to "seek after love and look toward the edification [upbuilding] of our neighbor" (3.19.12). We are free to love and serve others. This is how we should use our freedom, not to build up ourselves, but to serve others. If something we might do would be beneficial for others, we should use our freedom to do it. If what we do will not help our neighbor then, says Calvin, we should forgo it.

This is our guiding light: use freedom to help others. "Free power" is given to us in "outward matters." We have options on what to do or not to do. But power and freedom are given that we "may be the more ready for all the duties of love" (3.19.12).

62. Unburdening Our Troubles

> For prayer was not ordained that we should be haughtily puffed up before God, or greatly esteem anything of ours, but that, having confessed our guilt, we should deplore our distresses before him, as children unburden their troubles to their parents. (*Institutes* 3.20.12)

Though we daily recognize our sinfulness as Christian believers, we also daily pray to God. We acknowledge our "misery, destitution, and uncleanness." We feel "pressed down" and "troubled by a heavy weight of sins," knowing that we cannot gain God's favor on our own. We are laden with "many offenses" that can even render God terrifying. Yet we "do not cease to present" ourselves to God. Even these feelings do not prevent us from approaching God in prayer (3.20.12).

Indeed, a purpose of prayer is to unburden ourselves of our sins before the Lord. Prayer is not given to us that we should be "haughtily puffed up before God, or greatly esteem anything of ours." Instead, we confess our guilt, deploring our distresses to God, like children acknowledge their mistakes and anxieties to their parents.

This is the great freedom and comfort of prayer. We can confess all our sins, all we have done and left undone, all our failures in thought, word, and deed. We can confess everything, unburdening our troubles and trusting that God will receive us and forgive us as parents do for children. We do not have to play hide-and-seek with God. God hears and knows the worst we can confess. In prayer, God calms our anguishes, eases our cares, and casts out our fears in order to "draw us gently to himself—nay, removing all rough spots, not to mention hindrances, he may pave the way." All this is from God's "incomparable compassion" (3.20.12).

We pray in trust. God hears and forgives.

63. Wishing and Hoping the Best for All

> Let the Christian man, then, conform his prayers to this rule in order that they may be in common and embrace all who are his brothers in Christ, not only those whom he at present sees and recognizes as such but all men who dwell on earth. For what God has determined concerning them is beyond our knowing except that it is no less godly than humane to wish and hope the best for them. (*Institutes* 3.20.38)

When we address God in prayer we may do so on intimate terms. Jesus began his model prayer: "Our Father" (Matt. 6:9). The term immediately focuses on a relationship of love and trust between us and God. It also unites us with others in the faith since says Calvin, "we are equally children of such a father" (3.20.38). The parental relationship is what matters here. God is beyond all gender reference and relates to us in the closest, human terms.

So our prayers will be to God. They will also be on behalf of others who are sisters and brothers to us in Christ. We pray for the church and all its members. We pray for those we know in the communion of saints as well as those who are unknown to us, but known to God. This is a common core for our prayers, always.

But Calvin notes too that we should pray for all who dwell on earth. Not all who live have confessed faith in Christ. But no matter. How God will work with them is up to God. This is beyond our knowing. Yet it is right to "wish and hope the best for them." We never give up on what God can do. So we wish and hope and pray for all!

6. When Times Are Good

64. The Fountain of Every Good

It will not suffice simply to hold that there is One whom all ought to honor and adore, unless we are also persuaded that he is the fountain of every good, and that we must seek nothing elsewhere than in him. (*Institutes* 1.2.1)

Our Christian faith tells us not only that God exists, but also who this God is and what God is like. The Bible proclaims God as a personal God, as one who relates to us as humans in personal ways. The story of Scripture is the story of God's interactions and providing for people.

Our view of God is that God is personal and also that God is "the fountain of every good." This is not simply in a philosophical sense that God is a first cause and whatever we consider good in our value systems can be attributed to this God.

Rather, God as the fountain of every good, according to Calvin, relates to God's work in sustaining the universe, regulating it by divine wisdom, preserving it, and ruling and relating to humankind. God bears with the creation—and us!—in divine mercy and watches over us in protection. We recognize that the God who does this is also the one from whom flows all righteousness, power, and truth.

So when it comes to whom to thank for the blessings and benefits that we receive, the answer is simple: God. God does this and is also the "Author of salvation," providing reconciliation in Christ. The Lord is shown as the Creator. Then "in the face of Christ [cf. 2 Cor. 4:6] he shows himself the Redeemer" (1.2.1).

When we sing, "Praise God, from whom all blessings flow," we are acknowledging God's blessings to us in all of life. We are acknowledging God as the source of all goodness, in very specific ways. Praise God!

65. Feeling God's Power and Grace

> It is to recognize that God has destined all things for our good and salvation but at the same time to feel his power and grace in ourselves and in the great benefits he has conferred upon us, and so bestir ourselves to trust, invoke, praise, and love him. (*Institutes* 1.14.22)

There is a difference between having a belief *about* something and believing *in* something. One is the description of belief; the other is the personalization of belief.

When it comes to God, we Christians believe God has done "all things for our good and salvation." This is the most magnificent statement we can make about God's wonderful works!

But as Christians we also recognize that in our lives, we can "feel [God's] power and grace in ourselves and in the great benefits he has conferred upon us." This is the personal appropriation of our belief that God is working through all things for our good and salvation. We experience God's activities within ourselves. We receive the benefits of God's providence and salvation in personal ways.

This is the experiential dimension of our faith and why we can read Scripture, pray, and participate in the church in personal ways that strengthen and nourish our faith. We experience what we say we believe about who God is and what God is doing in our lives.

When our lives are full of a sense of the goodness and blessings of God, then it is time for us to praise and proclaim this God of personal experience. The benefits we receive lead us to trust, invoke, praise, and love God. Our gratitude knows no bounds!

As Calvin says, "invited by the great sweetness of his beneficence and goodness, let us study to love and serve him with all our heart" (1.14.22).

66. The Sum of Blessedness

Yet whatever earthly miseries and calamities await those whom God has embraced in his love, these cannot hinder his benevolence from being their full happiness. Accordingly, when we would express the sum of blessedness, we have mentioned the grace of God; for from this fountain every sort of good thing flows unto us. (*Institutes* 3.2.28)

When things are good it is easy to think that they have come to us naturally. Perhaps by my abilities or hard work or virtue I have been made to prosper. Yet this attitude is most dangerous. We know that all we are and have comes from God. God's benevolence brings us full happiness—when we live in the midst of "earthly miseries and calamities," or when life is not that difficult.

It is especially when we feel the goodness of God's blessings that we need to remember what is ultimately most important. "The sum of blessedness" in our lives—what all our blessings add up to—is "the grace of God; for from this fountain every sort of good thing flows unto us."

The fullness of all our blessings comes solely from the grace of God. God gives us what we do not deserve. No virtue or hard work or abilities of our own bring these blessings to us. Calvin says "the sum of our salvation" is that God has "abolished all enmities and received us into grace [Eph. 2:14]" (3.2.28). This is the basis for all our blessings, the free grace of God that forgives our sin and establishes us in the grace of God's community of faith, the church.

Put in perspective, Calvin reminds that "David sings of that divine goodness which, when felt in the godly heart, is sweeter and more desirable than life itself [Ps. 63:3]" (3.2.28). How blessed!

67. Gratitude for Earthly Life

When we are certain that the earthly life we live is a gift of God's kindness, as we are beholden to him for it we ought to remember it and be thankful. (*Institutes* 3.9.3)

In the good times of life, it is easy to think of the present life with thankfulness. We know our life comes from God our Creator and enjoy the benefits that we have been given.

But sometimes when we prosper we can fall in love with this life too much. We can look to our present conditions and see them as what we value first and foremost. They consume all our thoughts and attention.

In good times we should keep things in perspective. We know that our ultimate destination is God's heavenly kingdom. The blessings of life on earth are real. But we realize that they are not all there is. The present life is transient. There is eternity to come. We live in the now but anticipate the future.

Today we are blessed to "taste the sweetness of the divine generosity in order to whet our hope and desire to seek after the full revelation of this" (3.9.3). The blessings of the present anticipate the greater blessings of eternal life still to come.

But here and now we express gratitude for earthly life. Our earthly life is a gift of God's kindness and we ought to remember it and be thankful. Now we experience "divine benevolence" in receiving "benefits that are daily conferred on us" by God. This life helps us understand God's goodness. We are thankful for this life since God has "brought us into its light, granted us the use of it, and provided all the necessary means to preserve it" (3.9.3).

So we are grateful for our lives, every day. We praise God!

68. Recognizing the Author

All things were created for us that we might recognize the Author and give thanks for his kindness toward us. (*Institutes* 3.10.3)

To an old question—Does God love dirt?—the answer is given, "Yes, God loves dirt. God made dirt!"

This is a compact way of saying that God is the creator of all things. But it points to the physical world and all that is in it as gifts of God to us and for us.

For Calvin, a main principle of how to live the Christian life is to recognize God as the Author of all things. God "created and destined them for us, since he created them for our good, not for our ruin." Food, for example, was created "not only to provide for necessity but also for delight and good cheer." Clothing—apart from being needed for "necessity"—is also for "comeliness and decency." We enjoy the beauty of the natural world when we experience the "beauty of appearance and pleasantness of odor [cf. Gen. 2:9]" (3.10.2). We are blessed with physical delights that serve their purposes and are good gifts that are attractive for us and that we can enjoy.

In times when we find much to enjoy, we should see "all things were created for us that we might recognize the Author and give thanks for his kindness toward us." We give thanks and praise to the Creator of all, the Author of all goodness. We thank God for the divine kindness toward us that enables us to enjoy the whole panoply of God's good gifts.

If we misuse God's gifts in excess, we do not show our gratitude. We should live in moderation (3.10.5). All we have is from God. Let us recognize the Author!

69. Protection of the Parents

Now we must learn not only a more certain way of praying but also the form itself: namely, that which the Heavenly Father has taught us through his beloved Son [Matt. 6:9 ff.; Luke 11:2 ff.], in which we may acknowledge his boundless goodness and clemency. For he warns us and urges us to seek him in our every need, as children are wont to take refuge in the protection of the parents whenever they are troubled with any anxiety. (*Institutes* 3.20.34)

We often take the Lord's Prayer for granted. It is so common. We repeat it weekly in church, perhaps also daily in our devotions. The words are familiar; the form is ingrained within us.

We should be thankful for the Lord's Prayer every time we pray it. Jesus gave us this model prayer. It includes the elements prayer needs: God's glory and care of ourselves (3.20.35). In the Lord's Prayer we do acknowledge God's "boundless goodness and clemency." We praise and glorify God. We worship who God is, what God is doing, and the will of God that is always at work.

But Calvin notes that we are also warned and urged to seek God in every need, in the manner children relate to their parents. We are warned to do this because we cannot navigate life on our own, without God—just as we could not be safe in early life without our parents. We can take refuge in God—in good times and bad.

When anxieties emerge, we seek the protection of our divine parent. If our anxieties are not high, we may neglect the Lord's Prayer. Don't! We always need this prayer and the God to whom we pray.

70. Our Daily Bread

But by this petition we ask of God all things in general that our bodies have need to use under the elements of this world [Gal. 4:3], not only for food and clothing but also for everything God perceives to be beneficial to us, that we may eat our daily bread in peace. Briefly, by this we give ourselves over to his care and entrust ourselves to his providence that he may feed, nourish, and preserve us. (*Institutes* 3.20.44)

In the Lord's Prayer, we may pray for "our daily bread" (Matt. 6:11). No prayer could be more down to earth than this!

Each day we may pray for the resources we need. God is concerned with our bodies as well as the rest of us. We are able to use the elements of this world to take care of our human, physical needs. Thank God!

By extension, Calvin sees our daily bread as meaning not only food and clothing but everything God perceives to be beneficial to us. This enables us to have what we need to maintain our lives and be sustained. As we receive God's benefits in good times, including food and clothing, we express thanks that God knows our physical needs and meets them by graciously providing for us.

In a theological sense we are praying to give ourselves to God's care, entrusting ourselves to divine providence, so that God may "feed, nourish, and preserve us." Our petition is recognizing God as the source of all care for us. We live in God's providence. We receive God's loving care, expressed in providing for all our needs.

We pray for only as much as we need now. God meets our needs daily. As God nourishes us today, God "will not fail us tomorrow" (3.20.44).

7. When Times Are Bad

71. God Our Protector

[The mind] recognizes God because it knows that he governs all things; and trusts that he is its guide and protector, therefore giving itself over completely to trust in him. (*Institutes* 1.2.2)

We face many dangerous things in life. Difficulties beset us, both the kind we can anticipate and those that unexpectedly cause us troubles. We never know what is around the next corner.

Through it all, God is our protector. We believe and know that God governs all things. Life is not a lottery. God works for us and with us to accomplish divine purposes in our lives.

Even more, we trust God to be our guide and protector. This is the utmost in faith—entrusting ourselves in all the ups and downs of life into God's protective care. So we can fully give ourselves completely to trust in God.

God is also "the Author of every good" (1.2.2). God can handle whatever emerges in our lives and protect us through anything. All the goodness we experience in life originates with our Creator.

So we await help from God. We trust that help will come and protection is ours because we are persuaded that God is "good and merciful." We are not left wondering whether we are dealing with blind forces that can crush us. Instead, we rest in "perfect trust," says Calvin, and doubt not that in God's "loving-kindness a remedy will be provided" for all our trials (1.2.2).

These words of faith bring us comfort in the midst of all the difficulties and dangers that we face. Our hope and help is in the character of God, the one who has promised to be our guide and protector and who is at work in our lives in ways beyond our knowing.

72. Never Left Destitute

Thus it is that we may patiently pass through this life with its misery, hunger, cold, contempt, reproaches, and other troubles—content with this one thing: that our King will never leave us destitute, but will provide for our needs until, our warfare ended, we are called to triumph. (*Institutes* 2.15.4)

The Christian lives life "under the cross" (2.15.4). As followers of Jesus Christ, we deny ourselves and follow Christ (Mark 8:34) wherever that may take us.

It sometimes takes us into difficulties. As Calvin said, "While we must fight throughout life under the cross, our condition is harsh and wretched" (2.15.4). This starkly states the potential results for disciples of Jesus Christ.

But Calvin goes on to assure that there is help if this is where we find ourselves. He says this while considering the blessings of one of the three offices of Jesus Christ: prophet, priest, and king. When Calvin discusses the blessing of Christ's kingly office, he indicates that our ultimate happiness "belongs to the heavenly life!" (2.15.4). Heavenly life will be ruled by Christ and will bring perfect joy and happiness.

But even now we can experience the benefits of Christ's kingly office in a spiritual manner. For we can patiently pass through this life. We know a better life awaits. But for now we must endure life's misery, hunger, cold, contempt, reproaches, and other troubles—content in the knowledge that Christ our King will provide for us.

Our King cares. We will never be left destitute. We have "confidence to struggle fearlessly against the devil, sin, and death," equipped with the power and blessings of Christ our King (2.15.4).

73. The Certainty of Faith

If you contemplate yourself, that is sure damnation. But since Christ has been so imparted to you with all his benefits that all his things are made yours, that you are made a member of him, indeed one with him, his righteousness overwhelms your sins; his salvation wipes out your condemnation; with his worthiness he intercedes that your unworthiness may not come before God's sight. Surely this is so: We ought not to separate Christ from ourselves or ourselves from him. Rather we ought to hold fast bravely with both hands to that fellowship by which he has bound himself to us. (*Institutes* 3.2.24)

All kinds of things happen to us in life. The difficulties we face are many.

Resources of our Christian faith help us. We know that, left to ourselves, we face ruin. So we turn to our faith for an assurance that God is with us; the faith we confess will see us through.

Since we are united with Christ by faith, we receive his benefits. We are united with him, made one with him. We face nothing in life alone.

Christ's righteousness overwhelms our sins, says Calvin, and his salvation eradicates our condemnation. Nothing can give us more security in life than this! Despite the depths of our sin and sin's frequency, Christ's righteousness can conquer sin, and salvation in him makes us free.

Jesus Christ does not then leave us alone. He continues to intercede for us with God so that our unworthiness is not what God sees. God sees Christ's righteousness instead.

We are united with Christ by faith. This is certain. Christ is not separated from us, or we from him. This is our hope. Christ holds us as we hold on to him in faith.

74. God Provides Assistance

Paul teaches: "Tribulations produce patience; and patience, tried character" [Rom. 5:3–4, cf. Latin Vulgate]. That God has promised to be with believers in tribulation [cf. II Cor. 1:4] they experience to be true, while, supported by his hand, they patiently endure — an endurance quite unattainable by their own effort. The saints, therefore, through forbearance experience the fact that God, when there is need, provides the assistance that he has promised. (*Institutes* 3.8.3)

The Christian life is not exempt from suffering and difficulty. Tribulations come to us. The question is, How we will handle them? Will they deflect us from our paths and destroy us? Or, can they be met by a power beyond our own?

Calvin said that as Christians "we must pass our lives under a continual cross" (3.8.2). When hard times come to us, "thus humbled, we learn to call upon [God's] power, which alone makes us stand fast, under the weight of afflictions" (3.8.2). Troubles have teachings. We learn to turn away from "stupid and empty confidence in the flesh; and relying on it" and through our testing to find a deeper knowledge of God (3.8.2).

In the midst of tribulations, we patiently endure, supported by God's hand. We find that God, "when there is need, provides the assistance that he has promised." This is our hope and this strengthens our hope. God comes to our aid and then all the promises of God's presence and power are received.

The best part is that God promises to be with believers in tribulation. The promise of God's own self is incomparable. Nothing more can be imagined; and nothing less can help us. There is no substitute for God's presence. God provides the assistance we need, always.

75. Everlasting Intercession

But we do not imagine that he, kneeling before God, pleads as a suppliant for us; rather, with the apostle we understand he so appears before God's presence that the powers of his death avails as an everlasting intercession in our behalf [cf. Rom. 8:34]. (*Institutes* 3.20.20)

Christians sin. Our faith and union with Christ do not prevent us from doing what is contrary to God's will and putting us in need of forgiveness. When times are bad we may feel we have sinned grievously. We have been so unfaithful, so disobedient, so much less than God wants us to be that there is no hope. Our relationship with God seems irreparably damaged.

In times like these, we need a savior and an intercessor. We need Jesus Christ, the "only Mediator, by whose intercession the Father is for us rendered gracious and easily entreated" (3.20.19). He is the eternal and abiding mediator who comes before God's presence on our behalf. He does this continually for us. He appears before God in the "power of his death," which "avails as an everlasting intercession in our behalf." Only the death of Jesus Christ can provide forgiveness of sin. The power of this death—for us—continues to have effect before God, through Christ's eternal mediation and intercession on our behalf.

This is a message that reaches us, bringing us hope even when our circumstances are most grim. Even when we feel that we have sinned, and sinned repeatedly to such a degree that we are unforgivable, Christ intercedes for us. Jesus can and will intercede for us "to the consummation of the ages [cf. Heb. 9:24 ff.]." He alone "bears to God the petitions of the people" and he alone can provide the way to forgiveness (3.20.20).

76. Perseverance in Prayer

If, with minds composed to this obedience, we allow ourselves to be ruled by the laws of divine providence, we
shall easily learn to persevere in prayer and with desires
suspended, patiently to wait for the Lord. Then we shall
be sure that, even though he does not appear, he is always
present to us, and will in his own time declare how he
has never had ears deaf to the prayers that in men's eyes
he seems to have neglected. (*Institutes* 3.20.51)

Sometimes we pray and nothing seems to happen. In the midst
of difficulties we may be tempted to give up and throw in the
towel.

At these times, we need hope. Calvin reminds us that in the
Scriptures people persisted in praying. In the Psalms "we can
often see that David and other believers, when they are almost
worn out with praying and seem to have beaten the air with
their prayers as if pouring forth words to a deaf God, still do
not cease to pray [Ps. 22:2]" (3.20.51). They pray and keep on
praying.

This is a word that we need to hear. It is not easy to persevere
in prayer. Indeed, we have to learn to do this. When we submit
ourselves to God's divine providence we can trust that God will
answer our prayers. We must live with desires suspended as we
patiently wait for the Lord.

When we do, we can believe that even if God does not seem
to answer, God has never had ears deaf to the prayers that to us
seem to have been neglected. We should "not faint or fall into
despair" (3.20.51). For, "though all things fail us, yet God will
never forsake us, who cannot disappoint the expectation and
patience of his people" (3.20.52).

77. We Will Never Fall Away

Let us therefore embrace Christ, who is graciously offered to us, and comes to meet us. He will reckon us in his flock and enclose us within his fold. . . . From this we infer that they are out of danger of falling away because the Son of God, asking that their godliness be kept constant, did not suffer a refusal. What did Christ wish to have us learn from this but to trust that we shall ever remain safe because we have been made his once for all? (*Institutes* 3.24.6)

We may be anxious about our salvation. Calvin said, "While we teach that faith ought to be certain and assured, we cannot imagine any certainty that is not tinged with doubt, or any assurance that is not assailed by some anxiety" (3.2.17). We may fear falling away and losing salvation.

But throughout the Bible we are assured that God gives the gift of faith and also perseverance. God promises to continue to hold us even when we doubt. We need not be anxious. For "Christ has freed us from this anxiety, for these promises surely apply to the future" (3.24.6). Calvin lists many biblical references (John 6:37, 39; 10:27–29; Matt. 15:13; Rom. 8:38; and Phil. 1:6) from which we infer that believers "are out of danger of falling away because the Son of God, asking that their godliness be kept constant, did not suffer a refusal. What did Christ wish to have us learn from this but to trust that we shall ever remain safe because we have been made his once for all?" Another way to put it is that if we are held in God's hand, we will never slip through God's fingers (see John 10:28)!

In our darkest hours, we need not fear.

8. Anticipating the Future

78. The Defeat of Evil

To the extent that Christ's Kingdom is upbuilt, Satan with his power falls; as the Lord himself says, "I saw Satan fall like lightning from heaven" [Luke 10:18]. . . . And Christ, by dying, conquered Satan, who had "the power of death" [Heb. 2:14], and triumphed over all his forces, to the end that they might not harm the church. (*Institutes* 1.14.18)

The work of Jesus Christ goes on throughout the world in ways that we do not know or recognize. The Spirit of God operates in wider ways than we can imagine. The kingdom of Christ does not take shape in big, bold, and dramatic ways, but in the small and imperceptible ways characterized by Jesus' parables about the kingdom: mustard seeds, yeast, and seeds sown in the earth (Matt. 13).

Likewise, the defeat of evil, represented by Satan, is also occurring. This too is not in big ways. It is by the work of Christ continuing through the church: the preaching of the gospel, the care of the poor, the quest for justice, the pursuit of peace.

In his own ministry, Jesus said, "I saw Satan fall like lightning from heaven." Calvin says this shows that to the extent that Christ's kingdom is raised, Satan's power falls. Through his death and resurrection, Christ has conquered Satan and ultimately defeated the power of evil. Christ's work is twisting and turning through history. It is not a straight, evolutionary progression between now and the future kingdom.

But Christ is at work in history. The powers and forces of Satan are defeated by the work of Jesus Christ. The ministries of the church continue on our way to the final reign of the empire of Jesus Christ. Our work for Christ is not in vain. Evil is defeated. And Christ reigns!

79. Our Judge Is Our Redeemer

Hence arises a wonderful consolation: that we perceive judgment to be in the hands of him who has already destined us to share with him the honor of judging [cf. Matt. 19:28]! . . . How could our Advocate condemn his clients? For if the apostle dares exclaim that with Christ interceding for us there is no one who can come forth to condemn us [Rom. 8:34, 33], it is much more true, then, that Christ as Intercessor will not condemn those whom he has received into his charge and protection. No mean assurance, this—that we shall be brought before no other judgment seat than that of our Redeemer, to whom we must look for our salvation! (*Institutes* 2.16.18)

We affirm in the Apostles' Creed that Jesus Christ will "come again to judge the quick and the dead." There is a future judgment (Matt. 25:31–46).

Common perceptions of the Last Judgment are of ultimate bliss or horror. Visual portrayals in paintings and sermons inspire more terror than hope. The separation of sheep and goats—the potential for eternity in hell—are enough to unsettle even devout Christian believers.

But we should view the coming judgment from the perspective Calvin suggests: we are judged by Jesus Christ who has joined himself to us and is our Redeemer. The bond of Christ with believers—Ruler with the people, Head with members of the body, and Advocate with clients—helps us recognize that Christ our Intercessor will not condemn us.

Our judge is our Redeemer! We look to Christ for salvation. The one who knows us best, loves us most. This is our hope and comfort in life and in death.

80. Expectation of the Life to Come

> But [faith] is content with this certainty: that, however
> many things fail us that have to do with the maintenance
> of this life, God will never fail. Rather, the chief assur-
> ance of faith rests in the expectation of the life to come,
> which has been placed beyond doubt through the Word
> of God. (*Institutes* 3.2.28)

We have ups and downs in life, good times and bad. Our Christian faith pulls us through.

Our faith is centered on God and God's love in Jesus Christ,
known to us through the Holy Spirit. God's gift of grace in salvation, received by faith as God's divine gift, provides a certainty that no matter what life brings us, we are secure in God's
purposes and love. Calvin says that although many things in
life will fail us, God never fails. What greater assurance can we
have?

Our ultimate assurance of faith is in the expectation of the
life to come. This is our hope, which will never disappoint us.
Beyond all the joys and blessings and tribulations and difficulties that we experience, this expectation of the life to come is
always there, grounded in the God who will never fail. This
certainty comes through the Word of God, the Scriptures that
reveal God to us.

We can't imagine greater comfort for this life than the promise of God's unfailing provision for us. We can't imagine a
greater assurance than the expectation of the life to come. Both
enable us to give our lives in complete service and obedience
to God in Christ, empowered by the Holy Spirit. We can be
actively engaged in this world to carry out God's purposes. Our
lives are secure, now and forever.

81. No Fear of Death

No one has made progress in the school of Christ who
does not joyfully await the day of death and final resurrection. . . . He will come to us as Redeemer, and
rescuing us from this boundless abyss of all evils and
miseries, he will lead us into that blessed inheritance
of his life and glory. (*Institutes* 3.9.5)

With the press of the immediate we are always looking to handle one thing before we move on to the next. This is often the
pace of our lives. There is a constant set of activities clamoring
for our attention.

This is good insofar as we are living out our vocations and
the callings through which we serve God in Jesus Christ.

In our quieter moments, another perspective is with us as
well. When all our duties and labors are done, there is a future
to contemplate. It begins with our death.

Calvin says we only progress in the school of Christ when
we are able to "joyfully await the day of death and final resurrection." We can await our day of death with joy. This doesn't
mean that we seek to hasten death, but that we are not afraid of
it. Though it is an unknown to us, it holds no terror since Jesus
Christ has won the victory over sin and evil. He has provided
for our salvation. Our final resurrection is assured.

What Calvin says about awaiting the Lord's coming is also
true for our experience of death. We meet our Redeemer who
comes to us, "rescuing us from this boundless abyss of all evils
and miseries." Our days of struggle in this present life give way
to the final resurrection and, in Christ, our "blessed inheritance
in his life and glory." This is our destiny to dream about!

82. Companions with Christ in the Life to Come

I trust that devout readers will find in these few words enough material to build up their faith. Therefore, Christ rose again that he might have us as companions in the life to come. (*Institutes* 3.25.3)

"Whenever we consider the resurrection," says Calvin, "let Christ's image come before us" (3.25.3). Christ's resurrection is central to the New Testament and to our faith (1 Cor. 15). It is the assurance of God's victory over sin and evil; it is the promise of our future resurrection as well.

When we think of future resurrection we are staggered because it can mean so much. We can never know all the dimensions that will unfold in eternity. Since this is so far beyond us and so contrary to our human experience in itself, many, according to Calvin, do not embrace the resurrection of the flesh. It is "something too hard for men's minds to apprehend" (3.25.3).

To help us, Scripture provides a parallel of Christ's resurrection as we consider our own. At its simplest, we can say, "Christ rose again that he might have us as companions in the life to come." Despite all the questions of how this can happen, or all the theological meanings bound up with issues of eternal life and the resurrection of the body, in its most basic form it tells us this: Christ wants us as his companions. This is amazing! He rose from the dead; and we will rise as well. His resurrection makes our resurrection possible. Christ's resurrection is the basis of "the resurrection of us all." The result is that we have "fellowship with Christ in the blessed resurrection" (3.25.3).

Our union with Christ through faith is our strongest possible bond. This is never broken, now or for eternity. We are companions with Christ forever!

83. We Arise because Christ Arose

> We must hold fast to that fellowship which the apostle proclaims: that we arise because Christ arose [1 Cor. 15:12 ff.]. For nothing is less likely than that our flesh, in which we bear about the death of Christ himself, should be deprived of Christ's resurrection. (*Institutes* 3.25.7)

When we affirm in the Apostles' Creed that we believe in the resurrection of the body, we are making a stupendous claim. It is a claim that cannot be known by reason or logic. It is a claim known only by faith.

But in the Christian faith, to proclaim resurrection is not an empty and vacuous version of wishful thinking, some form of pie in the sky, by and by. Faith in our resurrection is grounded in the resurrection of Jesus Christ. His resurrection makes our resurrection possible.

This was the apostle Paul's argument in 1 Corinthians 15, the great chapter on resurrection that is sometimes called the spinal column of the New Testament. God raised Jesus Christ from the dead, his resurrection being the "first fruits of those who have died" (1 Cor. 15:20). To put it in Calvin's language, "we arise because Christ arose."

Christ's resurrection is the pledge and prelude to our resurrection. Today, in our flesh, we "bear about the death of Christ himself." Christ died for us, in our bodies, here and now. But in the future, we anticipate the resurrection of the body. Nothing is less likely, said Calvin, than that our bodies should be "deprived of Christ's resurrection." Christ's death and resurrection are one act; and the benefits of both are for us, now and forever!

Our resurrection hope is grounded in the reality of Christ's resurrection life. Our hope is built on nothing less. Because he lives, we too shall live!

84. To Gather Us in Heaven

He has claimed his heavenly empire; it remains for you
patiently to wait until he come[s] again as judge of the
world. For he has now entered heaven, not to possess it
by himself, but to gather you and all godly people with
him. (*Institutes* 4.17.27)

In the midst of his disciples, the risen Christ ascended to heaven
(Acts 1:6–11). The promise to his astonished followers is that
he will "come in the same way as you saw him go into heaven"
(Acts 1:11).

In his ascension, Jesus Christ claimed his heavenly empire.
For Calvin, Christ's "abode is now in heaven" (4.17.27). He is
in heaven until the "Last Day" (4.17.26; see also Acts 3:21). He
rules on earth now, establishing his kingdom in and through
and beyond the church. Christ is at work while we believers live
waiting "until he come[s] again as judge of the world." Christ
reigns while we wait and while we serve him.

But we anticipate the future shared with Christ. Calvin says
that Christ is now in heaven, not for his own benefit, but to
gather us all to him so that we can share eternity with him. Our
ultimate, eternal communion and community are with Jesus
Christ.

This is grounded in what Christ has done. For, "we have this
hope of our resurrection and of our ascension into heaven: that
Christ rose again and ascended" (4.17.29). Our hope, and its
promise, is secure in what Christ did and what he will do. Our
anticipation for the future is blessed fellowship in the heavenly
kingdom, with Christ and all the saints of God. Beyond this life
is the hope of heaven with all God's people. God be praised!

SELECTED RESOURCES
FOR FURTHER REFLECTION

Battles, Ford Lewis. *The Piety of John Calvin: A Collection of His Spiritual Prose, Poems, and Hymns*. Reprint. Phillipsburg, NJ: P & R Publishing, 2009. Originally published as *The Piety of John Calvin: An Anthology Illustrative of the Spirituality of the Reformer* (Grand Rapids: Baker Book House, 1978).

Beeke, Joel R. "Calvin on Piety." In *The Cambridge Companion to John Calvin*, edited by Donald K. McKim. New York: Cambridge University Press, 2004.

Calvin, John. *On Prayer: Conversation with God*. Louisville, KY: Westminster John Knox Press, 2006.

Gerrish, B. A. *Grace and Gratitude: The Eucharistic Theology of John Calvin*. Minneapolis: Fortress Press, 1993.

Leith, John H. *John Calvin's Doctrine of the Christian Life*. Louisville, KY: Westminster/John Knox Press, 1989.

McKee, Elsie Anne, ed. and trans. *John Calvin: Writings on Pastoral Piety*. The Classics of Western Spirituality. New York: Paulist Press, 2001.

McKim, Donald K. "John Calvin: A Theologian for an Age of Limits." In *Readings in Calvin's Theology*, edited by Donald K. McKim. 1984. Reprint, Eugene, OR: Wipf and Stock Publishers, 1998.

Wallace, Ronald S. *Calvin's Doctrine of the Christian Life*. 1959. Reprint, Eugene, OR: Wipf and Stock Publishers, 1997.